NDSU
D1713636

HENRY PEACHAM

His Contribution to English Poetry

A RIDER COLLEGE PUBLICATION

RIDER COLLEGE
Trenton, New Jersey

HENRY PEACHAM
His Contribution to English Poetry

by Robert Ralston Cawley

THE PENNSYLVANIA STATE UNIVERSITY PRESS

University Park and London

235585

PR
2329
P15
Z6

Standard Book Number: 271-01130-0
Library of Congress Catalog Card Number: 71-127387
Copyright © 1971 by The Pennsylvania State University
All Rights Reserved
Printed in the United States of America

Designed by Pamella Gecan

Illustrations by Henry Peacham from *Minerva Britanna,*
originally published in 1612.

To my wife
ELIZABETH HOON CAWLEY

CONTENTS

PREFACE

Some years ago when I was doing a piece of research in the British Museum I happened to read Henry Peacham's *The Truth of Our Times.* I was sufficiently impressed that I searched for a modern edition and found, to my surprise, that the book had never been reprinted since the original edition of 1638. That circumstance sent me on an odyssey through Peacham's works. By the end of my journey I was more than ever convinced that he had not received the recognition he deserved. I came to understand in part why that recognition had not been accorded him. With a man who engaged in so many kinds of writing and in so many activities, it was almost inevitable that he would not reach the highest level in any one. In regard to this, the attitude of the critic should not be that Peacham's versatility was so great as to preclude his being outstanding in any genre; rather, it should be that, in light of that versatility, it is surprising that he did so many things as well as he did. In other words, the positive approach is clearly the one called for. Perhaps it will be regarded as at least something of a test that the more I read and thought about Peacham, the better I liked him; too often, as everyone knows, it works the other way.

I should like to express my thanks first to Miss Margaret C. Pitman (now Mrs. Vincent), who graciously permitted me to photostat her London thesis (1933) on Peacham, and to take advantage of such material as I found useful. I am indebted to her especially in my first chapter where I have adopted the details of her thorough research on Peacham's life. I wish to thank, also, the University of London for granting me permission to photostat the thesis. Next, I should like to thank the distinguished editor of the *Journal of Historical Studies,* Don M. Wolfe, for his kindness in allowing me to reproduce in large part an article I wrote for that publication. I also thank the authorities in the Huntington Library for a photostated copy of Peacham's *Thestylis Atrata.* Finally, I extend my thanks to the committee of the Princeton University Research Fund for awarding me a generous grant which made it possible for me to go abroad to do the necessary research.

Robert R. Cawley

LIFE

Henry Peacham, Jr. is something of an enigma. He was a staunch Cavalier, yet he favored the Puritan ideals of simple dress and plain food. He was an ardent royalist, yet his highest praise is for a lady whose family were parliamentarians. He enjoyed the company of nobles, yet he advocated the principles of democracy. He pursued antiquities with a passion, yet few men were more thoroughly aware of what was going on right around them. It is hoped that the following chapters will do something towards explaining the enigma.

Peacham was born in 1578 in the parish of North Mimms, Hertfordshire. The date was established by Margaret C. Pitman,[1] who took a rubbing in the chancel of St. Helena's Church, Leverton, which clearly read: "Henry Peacham: Aet. 19, 1597."[2] Peacham's ancestors included sturdy Lincolnshire stock. His mother, Anne, was a Fairclough, "an ancient family in the Countie of Lancaster," according to his own testimony. He had two sisters and a brother, Richard, older by a year or so. His father, Henry Sr., held church positions first at North Mimms, then at Leverton in Lincolnshire, to which he moved some time after 1593, and was the author of a quite well known rhetoric, *The Garden of Eloquence,* published in 1577 and dedicated to Spenser's Bishop Aylmer. He died in 1634 at age of eighty-eight. There was a charmingly close relationship between father and son, reminiscent of Milton. The son pays his father a fine tribute in one of his emblems.[3]

Henry Jr. appears to have passed through the regular schools of his day; the ones he attended were in the St. Albans district and in London. The chief impression he brought away was a dislike of pedants, a dislike he kept all his life. One incident he records in *The Compleat Gentleman*[4] shows his early great interest in drawing, which turned out to be the subject of his first book, *The Art of Drawing with the Pen* (1606):

> When I was young I have beene cruelly beaten by ill and ignorant Schoolmasters, when I have beene taking, in white and blacke, the countenance of some one or other (which I could doe at thirteene and fourteene yeeres of age): . . . yet could they never beate it out of me. I remember one Master I had (and yet living not farre from S. *Albanes)* tooke me one time drawing out with my penne that peare-tree and boyes throwing at it, at the end of the Latine Grammar: which hee perceiving in a rage strooke me with the great end of the rodde, and rent my paper, swearing it was the onely way to teach me to robbe Orchards; beside, that I was placed with him to be made a Scholler and not a Painter, which I was very likely to doe.

He looked upon his higher education in quite a different way. After St. Albans, Cambridge must have seemed to him a terrestrial paradise. Here he could pursue at will those subjects in which he was most interested: history, cosmography, and cartography.[5] He is on record as saying that he was "ever naturally addicted to those arts and sciences which consist of proportion and number." Miss Pitman[6] investigated the college records and found that Peacham matriculated as a sizar at Trinity College, Cambridge, in 1592 (he was then fourteen), that he was graduated B.A. in 1595, and took his M.A. in the automatic English fashion three years later. Nowhere in his writings does he speak with anything but affection and respect for his alma mater. He refers in the highest terms to "that noble and worthy-minded gentleman Mr. Dr. Nevil our Master of Trinitie Colledge."[7] And he carried away a deep affection for his tutor, John Layfield.[8]

A few stories of a prankish nature from undergraduate days have come down, but those Peacham should be allowed to tell in his own words: he is reminiscing many years later with a college mate: "I was laid hold on in an evening, by our Vice-master *D.R.* for whistling in the Court; and I told him (and told him truely) I could never whistle in all my life; you made answere, No sir, it was not hee; for could hee have whistled, his father would never have sent him to *Cambridge,* meaning, hee would have made a plough-boy of mee."[9] Unfortunately the record does not tell us whether the Vice-master's dignity permitted his sense of humor to play; it is to be hoped so. The second incident is shared with the same waggish friend: "Let mee remember you likewise (said I) of another merrie accident when wee were boyes, and Sophisters in the schooles, when you, and two more of your old acquaintance, went one frostie morning to eate Blacke-puddings to break-fast, and wanting a penny of the reckoning to pay for an odde pudding (having no more mony amongst you all three) you venter'd on it, and spet out a single penny that was buried in the Puddings end; so that by wonderfull fortune, the pudding payd for it selfe."

For the next few years we lose sight of Peacham and can only conjecture as to how he was spending his time. In an undated manuscript which he may have written soon after 1603 he refers to himself as a schoolmaster, though an unwilling one.[10]

There is no question that the bid for patronage had already begun. No one in that age would have found it at all reprehensible; making a living by one's pen did not come into fashion until the following century. One of the people whose attention he sought was the king himself. James had issued his *Basilicon Doron* (1599) as educational guidance for his son. Peacham seized the chance to practice his art of drawing by providing sketches for the king's lucubrations, which he turned into Latin verse and often translated into English prose, giving quotations from the Bible and from Latin and Greek authors which bear on the text. This work has survived in three manuscript copies,[11] two in black and white and one in color. The second is dedicated to James himself, and the third, preserved in the British Museum, is the very copy that Peacham presented to Prince Henry.[12] This was his first use of emblems, a genre he was to practice so effectively in later works. That his efforts did not go unrewarded is proved by his testimony[13] that "I have often taken his Majesties [portrait] sitting at dinner, or talking with some of his followers." There is ample evidence that Peacham kept up a connection until Henry's early death. In dedicating *Minerva Britanna* (1612) to the prince, he writes of "having by more than ordinarie signes, tasted heretofore of your gratious favour."

It is significant that Peacham's first independent work was *The Art of Drawing* (1606), an educational treatise doubtless associated with the teaching he was doing at the time. More important still, he thought of the art of drawing as being a necessary part of any gentleman's training. Since he later speaks of the work's being "for the benefit of many young Gentlemen who were my Schollers for the Latine and Greek tongues,"[14] we can safely place Peacham in

London by 1606. The book is a most detailed set of practical instructions, with exercises on how to begin drawing the sun, a goblet, or beasts, birds, and flowers. It provides a picture as to how the human face should be drawn and presents an enlarged eye for close study. In the later version[15] he goes so far as to say that he hopes young Englishmen might be encouraged to rival even the Dutch and Italians.[16] The dedication "from my study in Kimbalton this eigth of November" is to the famous Sir Robert Cotton; and we must not put it beyond Peacham to have wished access to Cotton's fabulous library.[17]

It has been conjectured[18] that Peacham may have taken holy orders about this time, 1606. But until further evidence has been presented, this must remain in the realm of conjecture.

His next work was *The More the Merrier* (1608), a series of epigrams; it was a genre in which he was especially gifted. The epistolary dedication to "M. H. C." places him still in London for he signs it "from my lodging in Fetter-lane neere unto Fleetstreet, this 4. of Aprill."[19] Epigrams were, in those years, riding high, and dozens of collections were pouring from the London presses. Peacham undoubtedly hoped that he was taking the tide at its flood and that it might lead on to fortune. Fully aware of the long tradition, he here enters the arena of satire, but on the whole it is all in good humor. This work will be examined in some detail in the later chapters.

As mentioned above, Peacham expanded *The Art of Drawing* in 1612. Some misunderstanding exists that the work issued in 1612 is a mere reprint. Actually, this book, known both as *Graphicé* and *The Gentleman's Exercise,*[20] is over twice as long and represents a complete rewriting. For us the chief interest lies in that the materials are brought strictly up-to-date, a proof of Peacham's alertness; there are even some important changes of opinion.

In the same year *Graphicé* was issued, *Minerva Britanna, or a Garden of Heroical Devises* appeared. Peacham must have thought that he had discovered his forte in the emblem; after all, it combined two of his main interests, pictures and poetry.[21] *Minerva Britanna* is based on his own rendering of James' *Basilicon Doron.* He plundered his own preserves, but he converted his Latin verses into English. And he greatly expanded this work; there were only eighty-five emblems in all three manuscripts of *Doron,* and two hundred and twelve in *Minerva Britanna.* The upper half of each page presents the emblem (or design or picture), with a Latin proverb above it. On the lower half is the descriptive poetry (often two stanzas of six lines each, rhyming ab, ab, cc). Each page is dedicated to a different person. Latin notes appear in the margins, with some apposite quotation from the Latin at the bottom. It is an unusually well organized book. So far as we can determine, Peacham had in mind the general plan of Geoffrey Whitney's *Choice of Emblems*[22] (1586). He thought of himself as being something of a pioneer because he wrote in his "To the Reader" that very few Englishmen had ventured in this genre.[23] The emblem as a form so appealed to Peacham that he promised—a promise he never fulfilled—at the end of *Minerva Britanna* to so glorify English worthies "in another Booke."

In dedicating the poem to Prince Henry and in highly praising both him and his sister, Princess Elizabeth, in the hundredth emblem,[24] he little thought that in the very year the book appeared Henry was to die, and in the next year the princess was to depart for Heidelberg with her new husband. He had spoken[25] in deep gratitude of the prince's "gratious favour," and with Elizabeth he had gone so far as to refer[26] to her "By whose faire arme my Muse did first arise." The double blow must have been a bitter one, and he may have felt for a time that it was hardly worth pursuing poetry or seeking patronage. Too much, however, should not be read into his having let a year go by before making his contribution to the innumerable elegies written on the occasion of Henry's death. By the time he got around to it, Elizabeth had married the Elector Palatine, and Peacham consoled the country for its great loss by combining *The Period of Mourning* with *Nuptiall Hymnes* in a single volume (1613).[27]

Was it in search of relief that he went abroad within the year?[28] His principal objective was the Low Countries. The most important event of the journey, it appears, was his residence with Colonel Sir John Ogle at Utrecht, who was both soldier and scholar and liked to gather about him distinguished men of all professions, whose conversations Peacham found fascinating. He was later to express his gratitude: "It had been enough to have made a Scholler or Soldier to have observed the severall disputations and discourses among many strangers."[29] And "his table seemed many times a little Academy." Ogle made a profound impression on him for he returned to praise him twenty years later in *Thestylis Atrata:*

> And expert *Ogle,* able to command
> A *Xerxes* Armie, if that need should stand.[30]

Even that is not enough; he must add a note to show his pride in the relationship: "Sir *John Ogle* . . . a verie honourable Gentleman, and my especiall friend, with whom I lived in *Utrecht,* when he was L. Governour thereof, whom (as well for Honours sake, as his owne especiall deserts, having done great service to the States in the Netherlands) I could not but (in this place) remember." It must have been more for his scholarship than his soldiering that Peacham honored him. At least Ogle took no part in the campaign at which Peacham was present.[31] The latter's unlikely claim in *Thalia's Banquet* that he "hath borne armes"[32] may be excused on the basis of poetic license.[33]

Besides his enjoyment of stimulating conversation, Peacham was a natural born traveler, a true *scholasticus vagans,* as the following indicates: "The true taste of our lives sweetnesse is in travaile upon the way, at home, or abroad in other Countries; for not onely it affordeth change of aire, which is very availefull to health, but variety of objects and remarkable occasions to entertaine our thoughts, beside choise of acquaintance with able and excellent men in all faculties, and of all nations."[34] He follows with an account of a rainy evening as he was traveling through Westphalia "where I had lost my way" and, as evening drew on, coming upon a stranger from whom he inquired in Latin the way to Oldenburg. The stranger would not listen to his protests but carried him off to his own home, "where I never found better entertainment, or had more friendlier respect in all my life."

Peacham is most characteristically to be seen, knapsack on back, trudging along a country road, anticipating who the next person he meets will be or wondering what old church will rise up around the bend. We know from later references that he made his way through the Duchy of Brabant, was as far south as Artois,[35] and, like Goldsmith, wandered "by the lazy Scheld." He appears to have been at Breda after the signing of the Treaty of Xanten[36] (November, 1614) which ended the hostilities, and he probably returned to London soon after.

At any rate, he was back before January 18, 1615, because on that date both books he wrote while in the Low Countries were entered in the Stationers' Register. In the first of these books was a detailed account of the campaign he had followed, *A Most True Relation of the Affaires of Cleve and Gulick, As also Of all what hath passed this last summer, since the most Excellent and Victorious Prince, Maurice of Nassau, tooke the field with his Armie, encamp-*

ing before Rees in Cleveland: and the losse of Wesel, taken in by the Marques Spinola: Unto the breaking up of our Armie in the beginning of December last past. 1614. With the Articles of the Peace, propounded at Santen. In the way of these seventeenth century titles it is hardly necessary to read the book, especially as the book itself is only twenty-one sheets, all inclusive. The work is dedicated, quite appropriately, to Sir John Ogle. Peacham says in "To the Reader" that he describes things "whereof my selfe have for the most part bin an eie-witnesse." He tells precisely how both the allied army and the army of Marquess Spinola were made up, and explains just what the conditions were that brought on the struggle in the first place. Pitman rightly says that historians have not made sufficient use of Peacham's information. He was quite aware that the material treated was ticklish and he was enough of a diplomat to watch his step, "Knowing the danger in medling overfar in affairs of state and businesse of Princes . . . hath caused me touch somethings more tenderly than perhaps I would, desiring herein rather to resemble the corke by swimming lightly above then the hook by diving too deep to fasten myselfe where I could not easily well get off."[37]

The second book he brought back from Europe was *Prince Henrie Revived* (1615),[37a] a work he dedicated to the Princess Elizabeth. He says in the Preface that he finished the poem "under the aspect of that star of honour . . . Sir John Ogle, Lord Governour of Utrecht, my noble friend." At the end of the *Nuptiall Hymnes* he had expressed the fervent hope that a prince might spring from the union of Princess Elizabeth and the Count Palatine, and the hope was fulfilled with the birth of Henry Frederick in the spring of 1614. *Prince Henrie Revived* is Peacham's celebration of that occasion.

It was while Peacham was abroad that scandal was attached to his name for the only time in his life. A certain minister, *Edmund* Peacham, was accused of preaching sedition against the king. The irony is that Henry was a firm royalist from beginning to end. Edmund was tried in the spring of 1614. Under examination in the Tower he said that another Peacham had put those traitorous thoughts in his mind, had indeed left incriminating papers when he "lay at this examinates house." He described this other Peacham as "a divine, a scholar, and a traveller." If he realized that Henry was traveling abroad, this would be a convenient time to put the blame on him. Absent men tell no tales. Sir Francis Bacon was one of Edmund's examiners, and for some reason the king took a special interest in the case. Bacon wrote to his sovereign on March 12 "that further enquiry be made of this other Peacham." Fortunately for Henry, the matter seems to have been dropped there.[38]

It is probable that it was in this period, 1615–18,[39] that Peacham was schoolmaster at Wymondham Free School in Norfolk,[40] a position which he obviously disliked. His nature was better suited for the person-to-person relationship of tutoring rather than dealing with a whole class of youngsters. At any rate, in lines of his next publication, *Thalia's Banquet* (1620), he leaves no doubt about how he felt:

> *Windham* I love thee, and I love thy soile,
> Yet ever loath'd that never ceasing toile
> Of thy faire Schoole, which whiles that it was free,
> My selfe the Maister lost my libertie.[41]

Peacham must have been pleased by the reception of *The More the Merrier* because his next poetic venture was a return to the same genre: *Thalia's Banquet. Furnished with an hundred and odde dishes of newly devised epigrammes* (1620).[42] There are enough epigrams addressed to influential people to make it probable that Peacham was still bidding for patronage, perhaps as a release from the drudgery of teaching school.

Those years were taken up also with some concentrated work on what is probably his most ambitious book, *The Compleat Gentleman,* which appeared in 1622. The dedication, signed "from my house at Hogsdon by London, May 30," is to William Howard, third son of the Earl of Arundel. According to some accounts the Earl had engaged Peacham as a retainer in his household, and clearly Peacham tutored young Howard, as well as his two older brothers, at Norwich. The provenience of the book is quite well known. While traveling "in a part of France, adjoyning upon Artoise," Peacham was drawn to "an excellent Scholler," M. de Ligny. Ligny informed him that when he wished to employ young Englishmen he found that they were not educated to perform the usual callings in life. Peacham thereupon decided to provide a book of suggestions, showing his countrymen how the educational system might be improved. *The Compleat Gentleman* thus came to take its rightful place in the long tradition of the courtesy book. It is easy enough to say that Peacham adds little that is new to didactic literature. But it is safe to say that there is at least as much "new" in it as is found in most of the books on such "old" subjects. Professor Raleigh was quite right when he declared in his Introduction to Hoby's translation of *The Courtier* that Peacham's work was "the most popular book in Cavalier circles." And Sir John Hawkins[43] continued the story for the last part of the eighteenth century; he says *The Compleat Gentleman* was "in high estimation with the gentry even of the last age."

Peacham seemed fated to have those from whom he might expect encouragement and support die off. He had known the Earl of Dorset only two years when that nobleman died. Peacham paid him high tribute in *An Aprill Shower* (1624).[44] In many ways the earl represented everything that he most admired. While of noble birth, he had the qualities which Peacham sought in the gentleman of the other sense; he was religious, kind, charitable, sympathetic, generous, and totally lacking in pride, "the Epilepsie of our English Nation." It is to be hoped that the earl fulfilled all that was claimed for him, though a study of Peacham's complete works shows that he was fully capable of making a thing or a person stand for an idea, and if the person did not happen to be the whole of that idea or ideal, the liberty taken was recognized and allowed for in the literary tradition of the time.

In the ten-year period from 1624 to 1634 it is difficult to trace Peacham's career. Pitman conjectures, with good reason, that he was probably spending those years in country houses of important people, though we have little evidence of just what his particular activities were. We do not need to take seriously his saying that he was through with poetry when his patron, the Earl of Dorset, died. But the fact remains that he published nothing during the decade that followed. One activity that we can assume that he engaged in was the search for antiquities. If he took to the road while abroad, he more than likely did much the same at home. He had shown the interest early; Malone calls our special attention to a passage in *The Gentleman's Exercise*[45] (1612) where Peacham says that he was many a time and oft a diligent observer of town halls, church windows, old monasteries as the best receipt against melancholy, "to which," Malone adds, "he was much addicted." Burton and he[46] might have made boon companions except for the fact that Burton had the misfortune to be at Oxford.[47]

Another interest he pursued was music; it appears that throughout his life music was seldom far removed from him. We know of his association with William Byrd and John Dowland; he wrote tributes to both men. And he contributed verses to a book of songs and airs collected by Dowland's son Robert. In the earliest of his works extant, his version of King James *Basilicon Doron,* he has a madrigal with music in four parts which he called "King James his Quier" and which is written on the last two leaves of the codex. In a considerably later work, *Thalia's Banquet,*[48] he reminds one of his favorite pupils, Edward Chamberlain, of how often,

> With voices viols have we pass'd the day
> Now entertaining those weake aires of mine.

And in the accompanying note he says he has a piece of music ready for the press, "a set of 4 and 5 partes." One who did not feel music deeply would not have written of it as "the Banquets frend," the "Ladie of the Quire," the "Phisition to the melancholy spright," "Our Passions Queene, and Soule of All below."[49]

Another profession to which Peacham belonged was the most ancient and honorable of them all, that of the scholar; he had every instinct. Most of his dedications were to individuals who, if not scholars themselves, were deeply interested in scholarship. The earliest of his books, *The Art of Drawing* (1606), was, as we have seen, dedicated to the well-known scholar, Sir Robert Cotton. In dedicating *Graphicé*[50] (1612) to Sir Edmund Ashfield he says, "you are generally known to be a principall favourer of . . . scholership." He was obviously drawn to M. de Ligny in Artois because of that gentleman's learning and, if he deplored the fact that young Englishmen were not getting the right kind of education, he deplored far more their elders' failure to value scholarship as they should.[50a] When he wishes to learn more about the illustrious dead of Lincolnshire,[51] he converses "with a very honorable and learned Personage at his table." Even so late a work as *The Valley of Varietie* (1638) had the declared purpose of being "for the enabling of Ingenious and Schollerly discourse."[52] The evidence keeps popping up all around us.

It was doubtless in these middle years that Peacham married. This event is one of the mysteries of his career for it was long taken for granted that he remained a bachelor. This is his own fault, in part, because he explicitly declares in *The Truth of Our Times,* "For my part I am not married."[53] But one cannot help wondering how scholars interpreted an expression in the same work when Peacham refers to "I and mine."[54] And in a work[55] of the same year he has "me and mine." The problem is solved by two wills which

Miss Pitman[56] was careful to examine. One is the will of Jane Peacham,[57] the widow of Henry's brother Richard. In that will she said, "I give to Henry Peacham my brother in lawe and his nowe wife either of them xxs." Nobody knows what significance is to be read into the adjective "nowe." It may be that his sister-in-law was quite aware that Henry, with his free and independent spirit, looked upon marriage as a burden and his "nowe" wife might soon be his "then" wife. The other will[58] is that of Henry Peacham, Sr.: "I doe give unto Henry Peacham my sonne ten shillings and to his two daughters ten shillings a peece in money." That would seem to settle the matter once and for all.

Though these years may have been fruitless in literary production, they were not being wasted. It was during this time, when presumably he was left somewhat to his own devices, that he was assimilating experiences that filled his later works, both in prose and poetry, with fresh and vigorous figures. The subtitle of *The Truth of Our Times* is, significantly, "Revealed out of one Mans *Experience*." And in his dedication to the same work[59] he insists: "I often . . . considered the Title, which was *Experience:* now least the Porch or fore-Front might not bee suteable to the whole Fabricke, I begin with the *Experience* I formerly have had of your Friendly respect of me."[60] He wrote *The Art of Living in London* (1642) to give others the advantage of his own experience and to warn them of the city's dangers; he says that he is himself "acquainted with her rough entertainment and stormes," wishing to make it clear that there is nothing secondhand about the advice he gives. In the same way he speaks somewhat proudly, in *The Affaires of Cleve and Gulick* (1615),[61] of the events he describes, "whereof my selfe have for the most part bin an eie-witnesse." In *Meum and Tuum* (1639)[62] he gives us a picture which might qualify him to be placed in the school of "realists" with Nashe, Deloney, and Dekker: "They found Master Lime in an upper Chamber, sitting by a good fier in a Wicker Chaire, with three or foure night Caps, and an old Greasie Hat on his head, one foote upon the Tonges, in the Chimney corner, and the other on a little buffet stoole upon a Cushion, his legge many Times bound about with a rouler of red cloth." Since this work is largely taken up with the bickerings of Meum and Tuum, it was a Bunyanesque stroke for Peacham to make them hail from "Wrangle," the name of an actual town near Leverton where he grew up.

Peacham's long silence was finally broken by *Thestylis Atrata,* an elegy produced in 1634 on the death of his patroness, the Countess of Warwick. The poem by which it must be placed is, of course, *An Aprill Shower,* published just ten years earlier. The first impression one has in comparing the two poems is that the figures in the later one are much fresher, more original. This may be due partly to the difference in the two individuals who are being eulogized. The reader is convinced that the Countess deserves all the qualities for which the earl was given credit. Whether she was that good or not (and we have to accept internal evidence), Peacham succeeds in convincing us that the ideal was real. Certainly a part of his success must be attributed, however, to the experience of those intervening years, years of maturing during which he learned at firsthand the lessons which life had to teach him.

It is probable, as Miss Pitman believes,[63] that Peacham returned to London from the country about the end of 1635. And there he appears to have spent the rest of his life. One extraordinary thing about him is that his literary activities, if anything, increased in those last years. Though it is true that only three works can even pretend to length, the fact remains that he published ten items in seven years, 1636–1642, in other words, from his fifty-eighth to his sixty-fourth year. Three of those items were actually issued in the year of his death. In "his Epistle Dedicatory" to *The Affaires of Cleve and Gulick* he says that he has "beene ever a profest Enemie unto Idlenesse." His record of production would seem to prove the point.

Coach and Sedan appeared in 1636. It was confessedly an occasional piece. In "To the Reader" Peacham says he wrote it at the suggestion of a friend in the Strand who could neither study nor sleep for noise of coaches. The work is something of a *tour de force,* and Peacham warns us that it is not to be taken too seriously. In fact, it is one of those essays tossed off at odd moments, "I being at this time in hand with a serious and laborious work for the Presse, ere long to see light."[64]

This was undoubtedly *The Truth of Our Times,* which was published two years later in 1638. A part of the title was "by way of Essay," and in essay literature the work stands interestingly between Bacon on the one hand and Dryden and Addison on the other. Peacham's subjects are extraordinarily diversified and to them all he brings a mature and sound judgment. We cannot but agree with Malone when he wrote in his own copy of *Truth,* "There is a great deal of good sense in this little book."[65] Peacham wrote on such things as "Of Gods Providence," "Of Liberty," "Of following the Fashion," "Of Friendship," "Of Parents and Children," "Of Travaile," "Of quietnesse and health." Stylistically, this is probably the best book he ever wrote in prose; scarcely a page exists that does not have an example of some figure revealing a mind that has trained itself to observe closely with perceptive awareness.[66]

The Valley of Varietie (1638) is an *omnium gatherum* type of work. It is didactic in nature and is frankly based on parts of Guido Panciroli's *Raccolta* (1607), or rather on a Latin translation of it. Most of the passages are derived from the Ancients, and Peacham is careful to give his sources in the margin. The materials may well have been jotted down in some Commonplace Book; a habit many seventeenth-century writers followed. They often concern what we would now call "old wives' tales" and at times remind us strongly of Sir Thomas Browne's *Pseudodoxia Epidemica.* Peacham dedicates the work to Henry Earl of Dover, "since my last being at your house in Broad-street."

Perhaps his versatility could not be better illustrated than by the appearance in the next year, 1639, of *A Merry Discourse of Meum and Tuum;* it would be difficult to imagine two more different works. *Meum and Tuum* has its analogies with coney-catching literature, and its realism reminds us of Nashe and Dekker. The plot is originally conceived. Meum and Tuum are twin brothers, sons of Harpax the usurer. They are "two Footposts that dis-ease the whole Kingdome," and they are "two crosse Brothers that made Strife and Debate wheresoever they come." Their divisive tendencies showed up early and their distraught parents wondered how to get rid of them. They thought of making them soldiers, but then it occurred to them that the brothers would raise a mutiny and destroy the whole army. The background for this story is transparently Peacham's own Lincolnshire. Ultimately the twins are placed, but they make so much trouble in their positions that they are forced to leave for London, where they believe their chicaneries will be less noticed. Meum and Tuum take to the high road, the route so familiar to Peacham in his many trips to the metropolis. They go by way of Cambridge and entertain themselves by visiting the usual places, all well known to the author from his undergraduate days: Erasmus' study at Queens, Radegund's nunnery, the Round Church, and Barnwell Abbey. There are some sly digs at Cantabridgian education with its logic and syllogisms, though we know from other evidence that Peacham respected his alma mater and valued the education he received there.[66a] In one place he refers to "*Irish* timber, which no Spider durst touch," which reminds us of the legend about the ceiling in the College Chapel. It is not a case of two copy-book tourists, Baedeker in hand, viewing the landmarks; it is a case of two very real characters, scalawags though they be, exploring the sight-worthy objects in a great university. Having satisfied their antiquarian interests, which we suspect they shared with their author, the two brothers fare on to London and go to the Inns of Court—where else? Legal trickery runs like a theme. Tuum says, "We cut, nor picke no purses, but empty them after a legall way." To compare the twins with Bunyan's Mr. Legality is like comparing a satyr to Hyperion. Also in the manner of Bunyan, Meum takes "a Chamber in Theeving-lane: *Tuum,* a little darke roome, that had but one window, no bigger then a Cat might creepe through, hard by *Hell,* neare to the upper end of *Westminster-Hall.*" Law alone would not satisfy their thieving propensities; Tuum turns fortuneteller and Meum practices quackery, "to cure all manner of diseases and griefes by stroking the part pained and uttering some few words by way of charme." Peacham loses no chance to parade two of his *bêtes noires,* taking cracks at the rich and deploring that people are constantly jostling for position, even in church. Throughout he keeps insisting that men waste their lives in petty legal bickering; he knew from his own experience that his sister Anne went to law against her father and brother over a deed to her first husband's estates. With all their charlatanry, Meum and Tuum save time for London sports; they propose "to goe see a Beare-baiting over the Water." And they obviously have taken in another landmark, "The Tower where the *Lions* were"; they would not have felt right about leaving London without a visit to the "roaring boys." But leave London they finally did, to return to their native "Wrangle," where they discover that their father has died. Of course, they at once get into a quarrel over the inheritance.

The whole story is told with a sprightliness that keeps it constantly moving. Peacham's mind was reproducing the materials in an original way, and it is clear that he was enjoying himself in the process. The style keeps step; it has about it a freshness that commends itself to the reader as vigorous and creative.

It would be surprising if Peacham, living in those years, had not taken some part in the political controversy.[67] Appearing in the same year with *Meum and Tuum* was his pamphlet, *The Duty of All True Subjects to Their King: As also to their Native Countrey, in time of extremity and danger. With some memorable examples of the miserable ends of perfidious Traytors* (1639). The work was dedicated to Sir Paul Pindar, a well-known royalist. It is a Renaissance document in that Peacham bolsters his argument by citations and quotations from the Bible and the classics, including fourteen lines from Sophocles on patriotism. In his honest way he never fails to cite his authority in the margin. Considering that feelings were running so high at just that time, it is notable that Peacham takes such a moderate position. In the "Epistle to the Reader" he strikes a balance between ruler and subject, "one not being able to subsist without the helpe of another."[68] And he reminds the subject of what advantages he enjoys: "He shall live in safety, and be protected from injuries and inconveniences." He even quotes Queen Elizabeth: "God blesse you my good people every one, I will protect you all to the utmost of my power."[69] He further says[70] that a Prince should "governe with mildnesse." On the other hand, he never leaves us in the slightest doubt about what the subject owed for these favors; a man should be "faithfull to his Soveraigne and loving to his Countrey."[71] The King is the Vicegerent of God, and, as such, the subject must obey him. If he does not, he will get the tyrant he deserves. Peacham's strongest language is reserved for "our homeborne Renegado's,"[72] and he goes on to say that "by . . . homebred Traytors and Rebels, the Commonwealth is in great hazard and danger."[73]

Two of these late pamphlets are in dialogue form, and that fact alone may reveal something of Peacham's natural tendencies. The first, a short piece, is *A Dialogue Between The Crosse in Cheap, And Charing Crosse. Comforting each other, as fearing their falls in these uncertaine times* (1641). The tone contrasts with that of *Duty* because Peacham is not nearly so serious, and his attention is not so much on the political as the religious situation. The two crosses, representing Catholic and Anglican churches, are drawn together in recognition of their common enemy, the Puritan. Peacham's satire is directed against the latter. Cheap Cross (Catholic) is beset by two Puritans in high-crowned hats; one is Anabaptist, the other, Brownist. He complains: "The Brownists spit at mee as they come, the Familists hide their eyes with their fingers, the Anabaptist wishes me knocked into a thousand pieces."[74] Cheap conjures with other famous names of the time such as "Martin Marprelate, alias Penrie, Browne."[75] The Puritans were opposed to all symbolism, and Peacham's approach is through *reductio.* Why not, Cheap asks, file off the cross on the king's crown, "as they did in Boston[76] the Crosse upon their Towne Mace." So extreme was the prejudice against "cross" in any form that a London tailor of that name requested it be changed. If things go on, Peacham says, a person will not "crosse the street, but overthwart it." On the whole, the piece is moderate, quite in contrast with most contemporary literature on the subject.

Peacham would probably be surprised, if not disappointed, to learn that his *Worth of a Peny* (1641?)[77] would turn out to be his most popular work.[78] The thinking that went into it hardly compares with *The Compleat Gentleman* or *The Truth of Our Times.* It is full of advice on how to be penny-wise. So far as Peacham is concerned, it is just another complaint to his *own* purse: "One very well compared worldly Wealth, or Mony, unto a Foot-ball: some few nimble-heeled and headed run quite a way with it, when the most are only lookers on, and cannot get a cick at it in all their lives."[79] He naturally resents having to live "on the Trencher of another man." What he is actually drawing for us is the "Character" of the poverty-stricken. To avoid such a horrible eventuality, he offers his own "go west, young man": "You may find entertainment among our new Plantations in *America,* as *New England, Virginia,* the *Barbados,* Saint *Christophers,* and the rest; where with a great deal of delight, you may have variety of honest employment, as Fishing the Net or Hook, Planting, Gardening."[80] Peacham was not one to recommend the Terrestrial Paradise; leisure for him meant work. The book, as it was sure to be, is full of London life.

The next book reflects much of that same life: *The Art of Living in London, Or, A Caution how Gentlemen, Countrymen and Strangers, drawn by occasion of businesse, should dispose of themselves in the thriftiest way. . . . As Also, A direction to the poorer sort that come thither to seeke their Fortunes* (1642). This is, in spite of its title, another brief tract, full of sound advice based, as he says, on his own and his friends' experience. Some of the tricks are so circumstantial that they may have been tried on Peacham himself. The pamphlet belongs, of course, with *Meum and Tuum* in the coney-catching category. Avoid "beastly drunkennesse" or you are apt to have your "pockets pickt by Whores and Knaves." Use your spare time reading good books and you will keep out of mischief. There is no question that the piece was written in all seriousness to save the innocent from trouble. Peacham is on record as saying that he does not wish to make his mind a storehouse but a granary from which others may be fed.

Another pamphlet which, like *The Crosse in Cheap, And Charing Crosse,* is in the form of a dialogue belongs to the same year, 1642, as *The Art of Living.* Its title is *Square-Caps Turned Into Round-Heads: Or The Bishops Vindication, And The Brownists Conviction. Being a Dialogue between Time, and Opinion: Shewing the folly of the one, and the worthinesse of the other.* Opinion, like the goddess Fortuna, is seen turning a wheel, with Round-heads at top and Square-caps at bottom. Time merely asks her to turn the wheel and Opinion replies waggishly:[81] "All heads are round by nature, Square-Caps with their Cockscombes on the top, came from Beastly Base and Roguish Rome; and become the head as well as Hornes doe some of my followers." She goes on to declare, "Your Lordly Bishops . . . never did good in Church or common-wealth." That gives Time the handle he wants, and he launches into a contrast between the good Bishops and "your own Clergie, who have cast of [*sic*] their leather doublets and aprons and put themselves into long Cassocks with grave Silke girdles hanging to the knees." Then he asks the rhetorical question, "Who have built more Colledges in our Famous *Universities,* more Churches, Hospitalls etc. in any part of Europe, then our *Bishops* have done in England?"[82] Opinion replies that "your great Gor-bellied *Cardinall Wolsey*" pulled down forty religious houses to found his college in Oxford, "which he left unfinished." Time gives him his answer home in citing Magdalen College,[83] "which like *Euxine Sea* never ebbes nor flows with more fellows or Schollers then the founder gave and left at the first." When it comes to benefactors' names, Time mentions, among others, the great Whitgift and then the Archbishop of York, "late Bishop of Lincoln," in whom Peacham obviously took a personal interest.[84] In the end, Opinion is half convinced: "I shall have a better conceit of them [Bishops] then I had."

Dr. Harold Levitt[85] argues with some justification that in *Square-Caps* Peacham had in mind three of the Smectymnuan pamphlets, two by Milton, one by Bishop Hall. However that may be, another pamphlet in that same year actually uses the name: *A Paradox in the Praise of a Dunce, to Smectymnuus* (1642). Since this is one of the last tracts he wrote, it may be regarded as summing up his final thoughts about life in general, particularly because it represents many of his basic characteristics and attitudes. First, it places him squarely in the school of Erasmus, and, considering his great admiration for the Dutchman, there was no other school in which he would prefer to be placed. It is satirical but, for the most part, is good-humored satire. It is "light" in tone, yet we know from his other works that there is an underlying note of high seriousness. The "paradox" consists partly in the various meanings he attaches to the word "dunce." First he proves to his own satisfaction that he is himself no dunce, because, if he had been, he would have succeeded better:[86] "Had I bin Dunce, without question I had, long ere this, perhaps bin double or Treble beneficed, bin a lasie Prebend, or Deane of some Cathedral myselfe, or kept a fellowship with a good living to boote in some Colledge[87] or other, as long as I had lived." Then he proceeds to prove that he *is* a dunce for having wasted his time in intellectual pursuits. Like Martial, he might blame his parents for having encouraged him to be a scholar:[88] "And to say truth as our Times are, the matter is not great whither [*sic*] a man be learned or a Dunce, for he may come to preferment as soone by the one as the other, though he be but a Tradesman or a Mechanicke." At times he associates riches with dunces, an approach we have also seen in his other works. The well-to-do "dunce" will buy a scholar his dinner, whereas the patron, from whom support might be expected, will let the scholar go hungry. Though no profession has a monopoly of dunces, his satire is mainly directed at incompetent preachers and what he calls "Dunsticall School-Masters." He harps on the Puritans' ignorance; yet he goes on to say that the straight-from-the-shoulder sermon of a Puritan is preferable to one loaded down with pretentious learning and rhetoric. Obviously he has no Puritan in mind when he hits two of his chief prejudices at once, shallow clergy and impressionable women: "Whatsoever their Doctrine or their divisions be, if they be handsom men and weare pontificall Beards, they are much commended by the Faeminine Auditory."[89] Throughout the tract there is little animus. His sense of humor and his sense of balance qualified him to laugh at others and, better still, to laugh at himself. In the end, he poses the question, isn't the dunce the more intelligent after all? We know his answer.

THE EPIGRAM

Before we undertake to assess Peacham's contribution to epigrammatic literature, we must naturally review in some detail the history of the genre.

Probably no genre has had a more continuous history. The so-called Greek epigram alone reaches back to the earliest recorded times and comes down, virtually uninterrupted, to a period around A.D. 1000 or later—in other words, a span of at least 1700 years. The complete collection includes more than 5000 pieces, most of them written in the elegiac couplet. Though Herodotus refers to ἐπίγραμμα, the term is not used in its strictly literary sense in the *Greek Anthology* till the Roman period.[1]

Countless scholars have attempted a definition of the epigram and have usually thrown up their hands in despair.[2] The only two objectives which appear to have been in epigrammatists' minds have been brevity and unity of thought. Etymology proves that in its origin "epigram" was simply an inscription, written first on religious offerings, then on temples and public buildings in general, then on statues of gods and famous men, and on tombs. The fact that the "epigram" was originally an inscription predetermined its brevity. In time the scope was enormously expanded to include historical events,[3] heroism, tragic circumstances, and love; in fact, there was little in heaven above or on the earth below that lay beyond the genre.

Professor Mackail distinguishes four main periods.[4] The first is pre-Periclean when the epigram was obviously a popular form of writing. During the great classical age, comparatively few poets resorted to the epigram, one explanation being that the genre did not lend itself to profound thoughts.[5] A third period follows, beginning in the fourth century B.C., when there is a definite renaissance of epigrammatic literature.

The fourth period is the so-called Alexandrian, which culminates in Meleager of Gadara, who represents the transition to the Roman epigram. If the history is pursued into the Middle Ages, it may be noted that there was a reflowering in the Byzantine period of the Emperor Justinian (527–565).

Briefly, the history of the *Greek Anthology* is as follows. In the first century B.C., the Syrian, Meleager, formed his *Garland* out of previous collections, including epigrams from the earliest times to his own era. Luckily Meleager's proem is extant, and represents an early example of perceptive criticism because he characterizes each poet in the collection by an appropriate flower or plant. A Byzantine Christian by the name of Agathias (ca. 536–ca. 582) was perhaps the first to list the epigrams under subjects. His anthology (known as κύκλος) has disappeared, though his proem, like that of Meleager, is extant. In the tenth century Constantinus Cephalas followed Agathias' style of arrangement by subject and, as in the case of Agathias, his original collection no longer exists.

We come now to the two versions most regularly cited. The first is the Planudean, a work of the fourteenth century by the Byzantine monk, Maximus Planudes. He abridged and frankly bowdlerized Cephalas. This collection was first printed at Florence in 1494 by A. J. Lascaris, and was the only version known to the early Renaissance. The second is the so-called Palatine manuscript, which has been subjected to varied fortunes. It was turned up by the Frenchman, Salmasius, in the winter of 1606–1607 in the library of the Counts Palatine at Heidelberg. It appears to be an eleventh-century copy of a copy of the original Cephalas, unmutilated by the meddling hand of Planudes. Publishing difficulties and finally his death prevented Salmasius from issuing a complete edition, a task that was left to the notable German editor Friedrich Jacobs,[6] a name to conjure with in the whole history of the *Greek Anthology*.

Any attempt to characterize the subject matter of the *Greek Anthology* is likely to meet with as much success as the definition of the term "epigram."[7] Yet, it is worth noting some of the tendencies which the collection shows. As we might expect from all Greek literature, there is a leaning to be more general. Even where the tone seems light, there is an underlying note of seriousness, even tragedy. On the whole, if we regard the earlier epigrams, they are cleaner, less personal, less satirical than the later examples. Characteristic, too, is the emphasis on the Golden Mean, the Socratic "nothing too much":

> Ill-timed is all excess. 'Tis known to all,
> That even too much honey turns to gall.

This entailed being satisfied with little. A couplet of Theognis well expresses the thought:

> I neither wish nor pray for wealth; my prayer
> Is for a small subsistence, free from care.

And this attitude naturally led to money, the root of all evil.[8]

The serious note mentioned above, amounting at times to bitterness, is inherent. And it is therefore not surprising to find sixth-century Theognis[9] anticipating Sophocles in a famous utterance: "Of all things, not to be born into the world is best; but being born, as quickly as may be to pass the gates of Hades, and lie under a heavy heap of earth." And Menander fully concurs when he says that man and woe are inseparable. Perhaps the nadir is reached in a famous epitaph: "Dionysius, of Tarsus, lie here, sixty years old, having never married; and I wish my father had not."[10]

Actually, it should never be forgotten that the epitaph played a prominent part in the origin of the epigram. Certainly the essential brevity of the genre derives from carving inscriptions on tombstones. One of the most famous is that by the Alexandrian, Callimachus, written on his poet-friend, Heracleitus, which reads in part, as follows:[11]

> They told me, Heracleitus, they told me you were dead;
> They brought me bitter news to hear and bitter tears to shed.
> I wept, as I remembered, how often you and I
> Had tired the sun with talking and sent him down the sky.

One cannot read these lines and the "handful of gray ashes"[12] which follows without thinking of Milton and his poet-friends Edward King and Charles Diodati.[13] One of the greatest of the epigrammatists, Meleager, composed three epitaphs for his own grave! The range was wide, including memorial lines even to a slave, as Robert Herrick honors his faithful servant, Prue, or as one today thinks up a tribute to some favorite pet:

She who was once but in her flesh a slave
Hath for her flesh found freedom in the grave.

As the reader contemplates the exquisiteness of these epitaphs, he finds himself less surprised that they were used more than once, a practice that has led some critics to stigmatize Pope's undesignated epitaphs as "epitaphs to let."[14]

With this close connection between "epigram" and "epitaph," it is hardly surprising to find the epigram frequently concerned with the subject of death. Furthermore, it is not surprising to observe, the Greeks being a seafaring nation, that so many of these epitaphs memorialize sailors drowned at sea.[15] The great Simonides contributes only one in a long series:[16] "Lofty Gerania, evil cliff, would that from the far Scythian land thou didst look down on the Danube and the long course of the Tanais, and didst not dwell near the waves of the Scironian sea and by the ravines of snowy Methurias. Now he is in the sea, a cold corpse and the empty tomb here laments his unhappy voyage."[17] The vast number of such poems is surely due in part to the Greek's tragic grief over being buried away from his native soil.[18] How deep this feeling went is proved by the number of times it is expressed; an epitaph sometimes ascribed to Plato voices the wail of Eretrians displaced by Darius: "We are Eretrians from Euboea, and we lie near Susa, alas! how far from our own land."[19]

Perhaps the theme next most often stressed is that of girls dying before they have come to the marriage age. We recall how Sophocles makes a special point of this grief in some poignant passages of the *Antigone*. The height of emotion is reached when the girl dies just before the wedding is to take place. Meleager[20] himself writes a poem of this nature, describing how Death displaced the real bridegroom and "did Clearista receive on her bridal night as she loosed her maiden zone." He goes on to tell how the flutes were being blown at her chamber door and her bridesmaids were already knocking to awaken her for the happy occasion. And he concludes: "The same torches that flamed round her marriage bed lighted her dead on her downward way to Hades." A companion piece[21] speaks in the same note of pathos of how the girl attendants of Clinareta, instead of beating on the bride's door, beat their breasts, "as is the rite of death."

Pathos also underlies the epitaph-epigrams written on the young women who died in childbirth. One of the most pathetic of these is by Heracleitus[22] writing of Aretemias who had given birth to twins, one of whom died with her: "On bringing forth two children at the same time, one I left as a guide for its father's feet, and one I carried away in remembrance of my husband." But still more emotion is concentrated in an epitaph on a distraught woman who had already borne three short-lived children and who, because of "the heavy load of ill-requited pain," consigned her fourth child alive to the funeral pyre:[23]

> No longer shall this bosom find
> Nurture for those, whom Pluto claims his due;
> If I must mourn, I will not labour too.

The contemplation of death was naturally associated with the transiency of life. The *Greek Anthology* stresses this aspect again and again. Leonidas of Tarentum,[24] in imagery that is macabre verging on the grotesque, contends that man's span of life is but a pinprick; it is a memorable vignette in the form of a parable on pride. And just as inevitably, all this is associated with the evanescence of women's beauty. When Rufinus sends his Rhodoclea the garland he has woven out of beautiful flowers, he warns her against vanity by declaring that her loveliness will fade even as the flowers.[25] From this is but one step to Asclepiades[26] who, in language strangely similar to Marvell's *Coy Mistress,* bids his mistress to lose no time: "Thou grudgest thy maidenhead? What avails it? When thou goest to Hades thou shalt find none to love thee there. The joys of Love are in the land of the living, but in Acheron, dear virgin, we shall lie dust and ashes."

No theme is perhaps more constant than that of eat, drink, and be merry. The disillusioned Palladas[27] assures us that wine holds the forgetfulness of death. And in another epigram[28] he advises, "Drink and take thy delight; for none knows what is tomorrow. . . . All things are thine if thou art beforehand, but if thou diest, another's, and thou hast nothing." Wine is good for the poet; "who drinks water will bring forth nothing wise."[29] An epitaph[30] even calls from the grave on the passer-by to drink his fill before "enveloped in this dust you lie." This philosophy eventuated in the extremist view that the only good thing in life is wine:[31]

> The pleasure-loving cup of Bacchus fill;
> 'Tis the sole antidote for every ill.

The underlying note of most of these poems is naturally the scorn of the Puritan, Sir Toby's perennial rebuke to the Malvolios of this world: "Dost thou think, because *thou* art virtuous, there shall be no more cakes and ale?"

Venus of course was inseparable from Bacchus: Professor Mackail[32] skillfully traces the history of love in the epigram, finding mainly four periods. The chief exemplum is Meleager himself, in whom nearly all aspects of the subject appear. One hundred and thirty-four of his epigrams are extant; about one hundred of those concern love. In this regard Meleager is definitely exceptional.[33] Often he will associate flowers with the passion. And again he uses the analogy with honey. But the more regular association is the bittersweet one:[34]

> Love has something sweet to bring,
> But withal, past heart's enduring,
> Leaves a bitter in his sting.

At other times love is more violent than the seastorm, and Meleager goes so far as to speak of "the murderous deeds of Love."[35] Cupid is stronger even than Hercules, while in another epigram Meleager[36] rates him more powerful than Jove himself. The statues of Venus must often have appeared armed, for the inscriptions read that she who without arms had disarmed Mars needed no arms;[37] the present state of the Venus de Milo would have served the Greeks' purpose perfectly. It is perhaps significantly in connection with love that humor makes one of its rare appearances. Philodemus addresses Venus:[38]

> Oh grant me to keep my sweet mistress for ever—
> For ever—at least, till you send me a better.

If the treatment of love was something of an exception, the emphasis on ideals was more apt to be the rule. Man's mind was molded by Jove,[39] and Lucian was merely reemphasizing Plato's virtue for its own sake when he maintained that the wealth of the soul was the only true wealth.[40] After all, Menander had insisted that the one true life was living for others. To the Greek mind especially this meant living for the state. The crowning argument which Socrates offered to show why he could not try to escape was that he would be circumventing the rules of the polis. This meant that those who gave their lives in defending the state would be particularly honored in epigrams. The tribute of Simonides to the Spartan heroes is well known:[41] "O passer by, tell the Lacedaemonians that we lie here obeying their orders." And it is Simonides,[42] also, who, writing on the Lacedaemonian dead at Plataea, has left us the immortal line, "having died, they are not dead." The names are, of course, those familiar to us from Greek history, Thermopylae, Marathon, and Salamis. There is a particularly graphic epigram[43] in which the body of Leonidas is visualized as scorning the proffered robe of admiring Xerxes. To their sorrow the Persians knew first-hand the courage of Miltiades at Marathon.[44] The great Phidias erected a statue at the immortal site,[45] and we are not allowed to forget that Aeschylus himself fought there:[46]

> Let Marathon tell what feats by him were done,
> And what the vanquish'd long-hair'd Mede well knows.

Aeschylus[47] has his own praise for warriors in general, as does Simonides[48] when he apostrophizes "Athena's sons, in chivalry renown'd!" But it was Sparta which appears to have received most of this praise; perhaps the epigrammatists were partly responsible in setting this impression of the Spartans' character, which some recent scholars have questioned. The reputation may have been exaggerated —possibly by Spartan poets—because some incidents were dramatized. Quite a few epigrams recorded the story of the Spartan mother who stabbed her son Demetrius because he fled the field.[49] The adage was, return either with your shield or on it. It would be impossible to imagine any city where Falstaff would have been less happy. The philosophy that it is not death in Sparta to die, but to run away[50] is hardly to be reconciled with the discretion the portly knight showed in saving his own life.

No nation has ever paid higher tribute than the Greeks to its great figures, especially to its poets. Homer, of course, has his full due. So extravagant was this praise at times that Jove himself was said to be the author of the *Iliad* and *Odyssey*,[51] and Calliope was claimed as Homer's mother.[52] What he wrote is engraved on imperishable pages,[53] and, as the sun obscures the stars, so does Homer outshine all other poets. Perhaps what the Greek felt is best expressed in the famous lines of Alpheus of Mitylene,[54] where we are reminded that we can still hear Andromache's lament, witness the total destruction of Troy, and be with hapless Hector as he is ingloriously dragged behind Achilles' chariot around the city's walls. Nothing could convince us more of Homer's historicity.

Pindar was another favorite. The image of bees spreading their honey on his lips[55] may well have inspired the tribute to a considerably later poet, "honey-tongued Will Shakespeare." It is the fervent praise heaped by the epigrams on Sappho that makes us especially regret the pitiably small remnant of her poetry that has survived. Eight poets are mentioned and highly praised,[56] among them Pindar and Anacreon; then the epigrammatist concludes that Sappho is not the ninth among men but the tenth muse herself. As often as Anacreon is named, he is associated with wine, women, and music, particularly with the first. This goes so far that the poet's ghost is represented as appealing to passers-by to pour wine on his grave[57] and to plant vines over his body so that he might forever drink his fill.[58] Posterity's gratitude is, of course, for Anacreon's music; he is visualized as still plying his lyre even in Hades.[59] As with Sappho, it is tantalizing for us moderns to read what, in our ignorance, appears to be fulsome praise of Menander. In the eulogies the terms drop like petals: charm, enchantment, Graces, Music, immortal, heavens, siren of the stage.[60] He is a descendant of Cecrops, and he is now to be found dwelling with Jupiter himself.[61] One thing which a close study of the epigram may do for us of this age is to revive the reputation of that special correspondent for posterity, Simonides of Ceos.[62] When we have made allowances for the "graecomania" of Professor Mackail, his admiration cannot be disregarded when he characterizes Simonides' epigrams as

> among the most finished achievements of the greatest period of Greece; and in them the art touches not only its highest recorded point, but a point beyond which it seems inconceivable that art should go. They stand as the symbols of perfection in literature. . . .[63] [He is] the most eminent of the lyric poets. . . . Beyond the point to which Simonides brought it the epigram never rose. . . . His magnificent epitaphs are among our most precious inheritances from the greatest thought and art of Greece.[64]

Something of the poet's standing in his own time may be inferred from the fact that he, with Aeschylus and Pindar, was called by Hieron of Syracuse to form the nucleus of that distinguished group of artists at his court.

Finally, we should observe how the majestic triumvirate get due recognition in the epigram. Aeschylus wins high praise for being the innovator in tragic style and for his "eloquence sublime."[65] He is "Euphorion's son,"[66] and, according to what Mackail[67] calls "a well-supported tradition," he competed with Simonides in an epigram on the dead at Marathon. It is significant that one tribute,[68] however short, stresses the point that the dramatist was buried at Gela in Sicily, "far from his own Cecropian land." Even more ecstatic are the praises of Sophocles. He is the "Cecropian star of the tragic Muse."[69] He is a "God of wit."[70] The customary epithet is "divine."[71] With Euripides a particular convention appears to have been adopted with the epigrammatist's declaration:[72] "This is not your monument, Euripides; but you are the monument of this." In comparing him to Homer, Ion bestowed the highest praise known to Greece.[73] But the zenith of laudation is reached by Philemon[74] when he claims he would willingly be hanged if he could be assured of seeing Euripides in the next world.[75] The triad's contemporary in *comedy* found his spokesman in Antipater, who in a piece of acute verse criticism speaks of Aristophanes' graceful poesy that yet abounded "with dreaded wit":

Genius of Comedy! how just, how true to all that's Greek
Whate'er in satire or in jest thy personages speak.[76]

Of the masters in *prose* three stand out. Eratosthenes[77] mixes humor with his lines on Xenophon, calling him "wine-tippler" and waggishly claiming that all he has to offer Bacchus is an empty cask. An anonymous epigrammatist[78] made nice use of the fact that each of Herodotus' nine books is named for a Muse; all are invited to his house for dinner, and, to show their gratitude for his hospitality, each gives him a book. Similarly Agathias takes full advantage of the nature of Plutarch's great work, *Parallel Lives of Illustrious Greeks and Romans;* this epigram impressed Dryden[79] enough that he turned it in one of his finest renderings:

Chaeronean Plutarch, to thy deathless praise
Does martial Rome this grateful statue raise.
Because both Greece and she thy fame have shared,
Their heroes written and their lives compared.
But thou thyself could'st never write thy own;
Their lives have parallels; but thine has none.

Of the philosophers, Plato is naturally preeminent. "Divine" is the term used here, too, for he reached to god and heaven.[80] And the boast runs that, though the earth may hold his dust, his soul dwells with the immortals.[81] One well-turned epigram[82] has plausibly been ascribed to Plato's own authorship,[83] in which the writer addresses his "star" and wishes he might have all of heaven's eyes to gaze upon so beautiful a subject. But the epigram which Professor Mackail[84] characterizes as "most probably authentic" is the one which he further praises as "perhaps the most perfect epigram ever written in any language." By way of explanation, Aristippus has been quoted as saying that Aster, or Star, was a beautiful youth with whom Plato studied astronomy.[85] The following is Shelley's apt paraphrase:[86]

> Thou wert the morning star among the living,
> Ere thy fair light had fled;
> Now, having died, thou art as Hesperus giving
> New splendour to the dead.

And finally the great sculptors are not overlooked. In the case of Phidias, an epigram[87] "On a Statue of Jupiter in Olympia" assumes either that the god must have come down from heaven to pose for the sculptor or that the latter ascended to heaven where he might view the god. The tribute to Praxiteles[88] is even more neatly turned when it visualizes Niobe's statue; in the words of Addison:

> The gods to stone transform'd me; but again
> I from Praxiteles new life obtain.

We have spoken above[88a] in connection with Greek heroes of their participation in the famous events of ancient history. For prehistoric times it was naturally Troy which received the most attention. Always there was the chance to heap praise upon their greatest early poet. Thus Ilium, deploring its destruction, boasts that, in spite of all, its fame will endure through Homer's lines.[89] Another city to get special attention was Corinth, and here, too, it was the tragedy of destruction. Antipater of Sidon[90] graphically describes the ruins of her proud towers, the splendid temples of the immortals, the mansions of the wealthy in the days of Corinth's fabulous prosperity:

> There's not a ruin left to tell
> Where Corinth stood, how Corinth fell.

In our own time the line between history and mythology has

been demonstrated to be a fine one. And so it was in classic Greece. Certainly Hero and Leander were more real than Juliet and Romeo. The epigrammatist[91] clearly speaks of the lovers as having lived, visualizes the stormy Hellespont which frustrated them and the turret from which, like Troilus, Hero gazed seaward, the "treacherous lamp," and finally the common tomb. The literature is full of poetic inscriptions on favorite gods who were themselves half-men.[92]

The French are responsible for minimizing the satirical element in the Greek epigram; their critics implied that an epigram lacking in point was one *à la Grecque*.[93] Actually hundreds of Greek epigrams have a sharpness in their satirical twist,[94] and the expression is therefore a complete misnomer. A large part of Book XI of the *Palatine Anthology* is devoted to satire. What little may be said to justify the French caption is due to their possibly having restricted themselves to *classical* Greek. At best, it gives a completely erroneous impression of the *Greek Anthology*. It is true that the downright vicious element had to await Martial and Lucilius (who wrote in Greek and whom Symonds[95] characterized as "a Greek Martial of the age of Nero"). But there are many examples in the *Greek Anthology* of attacks on whole classes of society and in most of them, according to the poet's definition, a sting has definitely been left in the tail. All professions are hit: lawyers, scholars, and especially doctors. Here the bitterness really seeps through in such an epigram as that of Lucilius,[96] who maintains that even Deucalion and Phaeton were responsible for less destruction than Hermogenes the surgeon. Nicarchus appears actually to have concentrated his attacks on doctors; it would be difficult to pack more bitterness into a few lines than these:

> Marcus the doctor called yesterday on the marble Zeus;
> Though marble, and though Zeus, his funeral is today.[97]

Women, of course, took their pommeling, the male epigrammatists seeking their revenge for women's superior cleverness. Perhaps the nadir is reached here in what disillusioned Palladas[98] has to say:

> All wives are bad—yet two blest hours they give,
> When first they wed, and when they cease to live.

How can you say, the epigrammatist[99] asks rhetorically, that the hair a woman wears is not hers when she has paid her good money for it! "You have bought hair," writes Palladas,[100] "paint, honey, wax, teeth; at the same cost you could have bought a new face." The fool who ventures twice into marriage is like the ship-wrecked sailor who refuses to learn his lesson.[101] The stingy man is also ridiculed; the one who planned to commit suicide by hanging until he found the rope was going to cost too much.[102]

The poetasters come in for their fair share:

> The screech-owl sings its death-foreboding cries.
> When sings Demophilus, the screech-owl dies.[103]

Ever since Aristophanes in *The Clouds* made fun of Socrates, the scholar has taken a ribbing. Agathias[104] satirizes Nicostratus, a would-be philosopher who has tasted the wisdom of Plato and Aristotle and, "then wrapping his cloak round and stroking down his beard to the tips," he gives evasive answers on "what is the soul?"; then he draws the profound conclusion: "If you really want to find out, kill yourself"! But paralleling such attacks are eloquent defenses of and sympathy with the scholar's role.[105] Palladas of Alexandria is perhaps the best spokesman, being himself a grammarian by profession.[106] His war with life was due in large part to his detesting Christianity for overthrowing all that he held most sacred; it resulted in a philosophy as black as the city of dreadful night:[107]

> Such is the state of man; from birth
> To death all comfortless:
> Then swept away beneath the earth
> In utter nothingness.

But Palladas is only representative of a whole school. The epigrammatist felt it to be his province to concentrate within a few lines the quintessence of bitterness. Leonidas of Tarentum[108] is explicit: "A little life and a sorrowful is thine; for even that little is not sweet, but more odious than death." The corollary, sounding like a refrain, is that death is not to be dreaded but welcomed, death "before whom all human sorrow flees."[109] The thought is expressed in the form of a rhetorical question:[110]

> Why shrink from death, the parent of repose,
> The cure of sickness and all human woes?

The bitterness comes out in attacks on the rich, the usual resort of indigent poets to express what is actually their envy. The satirist Lucilius[111] put it succinctly:

A rich man's purse, a poor man's soul is thine,
Starving thy body that thy heirs may dine.

This kind of rebuke was normally accompanied by a lecture: "You are rich. And what remains? Do you, when you depart, drag your wealth with you, being dragged to the tomb?"[112] And this attitude in turn is often associated with the poet-scholar's declaration of independence:[113] "I am a poor man, but freedom is my house-mate, and I turn my back on wealth which insults poverty."

Now and then the satire is turned against other races, such as the one[114] in which a viper once bit a Cappadocian and died as a result, an epigram that reminds us of Bartholomew's declaring that serpent's venom was ineffective against Irishmen "because the greater poison overcomes the lesser."

The spirit of satire is the one element that brings humor into a genre which is so often sombre. Here the Greek runs parallel to our comic valentines. Growing a bushy beard was construed as an affectation.[115]

If beards long and bushy true wisdom denote,
Then Plato must bow to a hairy he-goat.

But the physical feature more regularly lampooned was the nose:

Proclus cannot wipe his nostrils when he pleases;
His nose so long is, and his arm so short:
Nor ever cries—"god bless me," when he sneezes,
He cannot hear so distant a report.[116]

Even more graphic is the case of a man who saved his life by using his friend's nose as a fire-escape.[117]

To all intents and purposes the Latin epigram is Martial.[118] He is chiefly known as one who insisted on emphasizing the turn at the poem's end. But about this, as about so much in epigram history, there is misunderstanding. In his fourteen books[119] he has many examples where there is no turn at all. Once again, it may be that the French are to blame. To them Martial is the perfect epigrammatist. Possibly, however, it is less his insistence on "point" than his indecency[120] that has appealed to them.

Martial recognized that the epigram was comparatively a low form of literature.[121] At the same time he is the genre's eloquent defender, claiming that the epigram contains more truth and human nature than epic or tragedy.[122]

When we try to sense the tone of Martial, we have to agree with Pliny the Younger, who said that he was full of wit and gall. This wit operates at times like the crack of a whip, with a telling turn at the epigram's end. When Cosconius complained that his poems were too long, Martial replied:[123]

> Things are not long where we can nothing spare:
> But, Coscus, e'en thy distichs tedious are.

His sharpness reminds us often of Dean Swift. He defends his indecency by citing his model Catullus.[124] As for his subjects, he complains constantly of poverty. As a poet today might deplore the million dollars a famous prize fighter could get for a single bout, so Martial[125] resents it that Scorpus, "a winner of the race bears off fifteen bags of gleaming gold" in a single hour, whereas he himself earns a paltry hundred farthings in a whole day. A man stops him in the Roman street[126] and asks him if he is the famous poet; then why does he wear so threadbare a cloak? He is forced to live in a third-storey garret.[127] And his furniture is so shabby that he invites his guests to bring their own.[128] With conscious hyperbole he describes his tiny suburban farm which an ant could eat up in a single day and where even a single cucumber cannot lie straight.[129] The poet writing a complaint to his purse is sure to appreciate, especially, invitations to dinner; and Martial has more than his quota of such appeals.[130] He naturally resents the practice of a host's eating better food than his guests: "The golden turtledove fills your stomach with its over-fattened body; a magpie which died in its cage is set before me."[131] How much food meant to Martial is evidenced from the loving care with which he describes what he was, on occasion, able to offer his friends. He writes,[132] though with tongue in cheek, of lettuce and leeks, tunny and eggs, cauliflower, sausages, snow-white porridge, bacon, raisins, chestnuts, and olives. Obviously his guest is going to enjoy an *embarras de richesses*. But another practice which Martial resented was that of guests taking home surplus food in their napkins.[133]

Actually, however, the theme of the simple life is more predominant in Martial. This may be due to his upbringing in provincial Bilbilis in Spain. All through the thirty-four trying years in the hurly-burly of Rome he longed for the quiet fields and uplands of his native place, through which flowed the pleasant Salo.[134] He could not know that he was to experience the usual disillusionment of anyone returning to his boyhood home; even Shakespeare's return to New Place must have had its sobering side. But while in Rome Bilbilis seemed to Martial like the Terrestrial Paradise. He deplored the disturbing noises of the city, the early morning shouts of the nearby schoolmaster, the hammers of the coppersmiths, the drunken sailors. Rome, he bewails, "is at my bed's head." He yearns for the simple life,[135] with "a wife not too learned, nights with sleep, days without strife." He contrasts "Manius, dear to me from my ingenuous years"[136] with some of the fair-weather friends he knew in the city. The homesickness comes through in the very way he mouths his favorite places,[137] Vadavero, Botrodus, Congedus, Voberca, "fresh Dercenna," "the sunny shores of Tarraco and thine own Laletania." These names are more than euphonious. There is something pathetic about his commending to Marius the care of his little Nomentan farm[138] and, as he is just embarking for Spain, about his sending a message home commissioning Flavus to provide him with some humble retreat, "which may make a lazy man" of him.[139] Once there, he twits his friend Juvenal in his sweaty toga toilsomely plodding up the Roman hill to pay court to some rich patron while he, Martial, sleeps late and wakes to be fed before a blazing fire by his bailiff's wife.[140] But then the usual experience. He senses the jealousy on the part of some of his fellow townsmen, and Rome begins to take on advantages; he thinks of the stimulating conversations, of the libraries and theatres "where pleasure is a student without knowing it." In fact, he informs Priscus at the time of that gentleman's projected visit to Spain in the winter of A.D. 101 that his life has become so boring that he has been able to compose nothing for the past three years—the boredom of an alert mind in provincial surroundings.[141] Similarly, when he addresses his good friend and namesake Julius Martialis,[142] he concedes, in retrospect, that the good outweighed the bad.

As with most epigrammatists, it is not easy to say what were Martial's special topics. Certainly his poverty led him to refer often to sesterces. And it was his lack of them that made him curry patronage. Domitian's name comes in almost like a refrain. Book VIII is grandiloquently dedicated to "The Emperor Domitianus, Caesar Augustus, Germanicus, Dacicus."[143] And Books IV, V, and VII open with similar dedications, or what amounts to that. In fact, the whole volume has for preface "On the Public Shows of Domitian." Yet the poet turns on him almost before his body is cold in the grave, and praises Nerva who "under a hard prince and in evil times, didst have courage to be good."[144]

It may have been partly this reach for patronage that made Martial praise his own work to convince others that he was worthy of support. Even Domitian, he says, takes time out of his busy day to read him.[145] As Verona could be proud of its Catullus, Mantua of its Virgil, so Bilbilis might well be proud of Martial.[146] "I am your glory and repute," he boasts.[147] Several times he notes that his verses are read throughout the world, in Vienna and even in distant Britain. And in the streets of Rome, people point at him as the famous poet.[148] The "gilded monuments of princes" theme is recurrent.[149] To be sure, he says humorously he could do with less praise and more money; a poet can starve on praise.[150] It is significant that, his popularity being so great, many should appeal to him for copies of his books; and his answer usually was, "You can buy a copy at the booksellers."[151]

Martial insists that he attacks vices, not persons. "I will not say, however closely you press me, who is the Postumus of my book."[152] But one cannot help wondering whether in the eyes of Romans his Sextus, Pamphilus, and Quintus were not transparent covers for individuals. To a certain extent this is true also when he comes to satirize the professions. Like the Greeks he lampoons the doctors, lawyers, barbers, poetasters, and, of course, the oldest profession of them all. He is hardest possibly on lawyers, perhaps because he practiced law himself, and presumably knew it best.

He has his quota of epigrams on history, on Cicero, Antony, Pompey, and Portia, on Ravenna and Vesuvius. Of the last-named he writes mournfully of the natural beauty of its slopes which "now lie buried in flames and sad ashes."[153] Similarly, mythology is well represented, with Leda and Bacchus, Mercury, and Priapus. Martial would not be a Roman poet if he were free from homosexuality; contemporaries would not have thought the matter worth commenting on. As for subjects that we might miss, there are, in light of the genre's origin, fewer elegies than we might expect, and, considering Meleager and his admired Catullus, certainly fewer love poems.[154]

PEACHAM AND THE EPIGRAM: MATTER

In many ways the epigram perfectly suited the genius of Henry Peacham. As we have seen, it was perhaps his curse that his interests should have been so varied. A man who had more than an amateur's hand in painting, engraving, drawing, heraldry, music, mathematics, antiquities, and cosmography, among other things, could hardly be expected to compose an epic poem. But the epigram lent itself admirably to those interim moments when the poetic fit was on. It is doubtful whether any form lends itself more naturally to the individual's voicing his present thoughts more sincerely. Martial had declared that there was more truth to life in epigrams than in all the epics put together.[1] Peacham was quite aware of the genre's humble status. In "To the Reader," preceding *The More the Merrier*,[2] he writes:[3] "You cannot esteeme lighter of this stuffe then I doe my selfe." And the whole implication of "Ad Musas"[4] is that the epigram is comparatively a low class of poetry; therefore, he can hardly presume to ask aid of the Muses.[5] He certainly knew that the literary giants of the previous century had seldom stooped to indulge in the form. A printer once told him that epigrams were "out of request"; but that has the air of a publisher's dodge, since there were at least fifty collections published in the first quarter of the seventeenth century, and both *The More the Merrier* (1608) and *Thalia's Banquet* (1620), it is to be noted, fall within those years.[6]

If Peacham was fully conscious of the epigram's humble rating, he was at the same time aware of its long tradition. So good a scholar of the classics could not help being familiar with the two-thousand-year-old *Greek Anthology*;[7] poem after poem takes our minds back to that famous collection.[8] He was, of course, equally acquainted with Martial and the neo-Latin epigram.[9] If something of the spirit and vast range of subject matter of the Greeks permeates his verse, much of Martial's critical sharpness, near bitterness, coexists, though, as Miss Pitman says, he did his best to escape from the Latin model.

That vast range may be seen in a survey of the collections. Whether he knew it or not, Peacham has presented us in *The More the Merrier, Thalia's Banquet,* and *Minerva Britanna*[10] with a fairly complete self-portrait. In the first place, there may well be an element of pretense in his tendency to belittle himself. In Emblem 101 of *Minerva* he speaks of his "worthles *Poesie,*" and, certainly with tongue-in-cheek, he visualizes his adverse critic, in a wicker chair drawn up before the fire, declaiming:[11]

> This Author hath some wit,
> Pitty hee made no better use of it.

Waggishly he may be recalling Martial's retort to the impertinent questioner who asked him why his toga was so poor: "Because I am a poor poet." But there are qualities more basic than this. In the very period when democracy was fighting its way up through a welter of privilege, he cast his lot with the self-deserving. Conceivably lifting the idea from Ovid, but obviously with full approval, he praises the men[12]

> Who not of Fathers Actes ambitious are
> But of the brave Atcheivements of their owne.

In the much later *Thestylis Atrata,*[13] he writes:

> But what availes all this, it is not Bloud,
> Alliance, Honours, Fortunes make us good:
> These are but rind, or out-side seeming faire,
> Which toucht, will turne to ashes or to aire.

The "meaner wight," he insists,[14] "many times in vertue doth excell." And the Norfolk yeoman who dared to ask him how he might come by a coat of arms got his answer home:[15] "Desert, quoth I, must winne gentility." In fact, he constantly wondered over men's "foolish thirsting after Names, Honors and Titles."[16]

This conviction was associated with an even deeper feeling about man's retaining his individuality and independence.[16a] If one had to pick a single characteristic of Peacham that predominated, this would be it; all other traits appear to stem from it. Of many expressions perhaps the best is in *Minerva Britanna:*[17]

> The meaning is, the wise and valiant mind,
> In Povertie esteemes not Fate a straw
> And libertie to live, not like a slave
> Here in this world, she little else doth lack:
> But can contented in her cottage sing,
> In greater safetie, then the greatest King.[18]

Similarly he contends[19] that it is hell to live like a caged bird "at others curt'sie" whereas all he asks is to be kept from cold and hunger. I would rather, he says, eat at a three-penny Ordinary than to be a dumb tenant for two hours at a Lord's table.[20] This reaches naturally to his poetry, which he refuses to prostitute in praising the unworthy man, "that's empty of Desert."[21]

Connected as well with the above is Peacham's deploring that rewards go to men of position and wealth rather than to those who really deserve them (obviously he has himself in mind!);[22] and he emphasizes the spurns that patient merit of the unworthy takes. He weeps that so many men of rarest parts are not afforded a single foothold by an ungrateful world.[23] Like bees, those who have striven hardest for the hive must stand aside and watch inferior workers prosper.[24] Perhaps the bitterest expression of all comes in the epigram where a man gives up winning by desert, and finds that he can go further by turning fool.[25] The same idea is voiced in *Minerva Britanna:*[26]

> Who seekst Promotion through just desert,
> And thinkst by gift of bodie, or of mind,
> To raise thy fortune, whosoere thou art,
> This new *Impresa* take to thee assign'd.
> To warne thee oft, such labour is in vaine,
> If hereby thinkst thy merit to obtaine.
>
> . . . .
>
> Such is our age, where virtue's scarce regarded
> And artes with armes must wander unrewarded.[27]

This note runs like a refrain through *Minerva Britanna.* He will speak from the heart of the cold and frozen respect of learning and the arts, of how ill those same arts fare,[28] of how learning and the arts formerly flourished,[29] now "wash'd and worne" by the very people who should have upheld them.[30] This matter of the lack of dependable patrons distresses him:[31]

> The rich with Bountie should rewarde the Artes,
> The living muse should gratefully againe,
> Adorne Maecenas with her learned partes:
> And when his branch is drie, and withered seene,
> By her support, preserve him always greene.

Actually Peacham's verse is reasonably full of tributes to patrons,[32] and though he protests[33] that he will not "guild or reare my friends beyond desert," he proceeds to do so. From Prince Henry down he has some tolerably fulsome praise. You will never, he assures one generous benefactor, be able to say that you gave your gold to "one unthankfull."[34]

Conceivably there is an element of rationalization in his maintaining that poverty and virtue go hand-in-hand. "Povertie," he records in *The Valley of Varietie,*[35] quoting Petronius with obvious approval, "is alwaies the Sister of a vertuous, or honest mind." This also was a theme to which he paid much more than lip service; he reminds his friend John Browne that[36]

> . . . the fountaine is the mind.
> . . . .
> Lay your foundation sure, the heavenly *feare*
> And pure *religion,* hereon let be pight,
> Your lives strong frame that's *honest* and *upright*
> . . . a conscience cleere of sin.

He highly praises[37] the parents of a lady whose life has been a model because they laid the foundation of her character in true religion "and hence that goodly structure of her minde proceeded."[38]

In the matter of religion Peacham stands where we might expect; true son of the Renaissance, he was a moderate in a period of religious extremes. Admittedly he assails the Puritan zealots in *The Duty of All True Subjects to Their King* (1639), *Square-Caps Turned into Round-Heads* (1642), and *A Dialogue between the Crosse in Cheap and Charing Crosse* (1641);[39] but at the same time he deplores the lavish ceremony practiced in some established churches. And he certainly has little sympathy with the extravagance at court, the elaborate feasting and fantastic dress. More to his liking are the sparse provisions of college commons and the simple dress of the

Puritans.[40] In *A Dialogue* he makes little choice between Charing Cross and the Catholic Cross[41] at Cheap, contending that both have been equally subject to the ridiculous attacks of Martin Marprelate. As for moderation in general,[42] there may be some significance in his having chosen to include "Temperantia" among his emblems: "Heere *Temperance* I stand, of virtues Queene."

Miss Pitman has rightly characterized Peacham as a moderate royalist. The rather vicious attack on the bigoted Puritan in *Minerva Britanna* concludes with the line, "And Pride presumes to overlooke his King." There can be no question that a strong patriotic strain runs through Peacham. If it can be said that his addressing the first emblem of *Minerva Britanna* to King James has in it an element of the conventional,[43] the 108th, entitled "Ad Britanniam," with its use of history has considerably more:

> Usurping *Rome* standes now in aw of thee:
> And trembles more to heare thy Soveraignes name
> Then thou her Drummes when valiant *Caesar* came.

Similarly British kings and heroes "who served *Eliza* in her raigne" are eulogized in emblem 208. And he swears vengeance[44] on "them that shall abuse th' anointed Diadem" since "Diadem's of Princes ever yet, from base controule, have beene exempt and free."[45]

If he was loyal to his sovereign, he was similarly loyal to his alma mater, for which he retained a singular fondness; in an emblem[46] addressed to a fellow of Trinity College, Cambridge, he shows this affection for what he elsewhere[47] calls "my ever-loved Mother." The same sentiments are expressed in *Thalia's Banquet:*[48]

> So let me Sir of heaven beloved bee,
> As I do love my Nurse your Trinitie;
> Whereof I was a member, bleeding yet,
> To thinke how rawlie I was torne from it:
> But wholy not divided though in part,
> Since (fellowes) yet amongst you lives my heart.

The "rawlie" torn from it probably means nothing more than is explained in a slightly later epigram where he is also praising Cambridge:[49]

> Oh were it not that some are wean'd too young,
> And some do suck (like *Essex* calves) too long!

In other words, he is merely voicing the common experience of a student who comes to graduation feeling that there are other valuable studies he might have pursued.

Naturally his birthplace comes in for its meed of praise. Peacham appears to have looked nostalgically upon North Mimms, just as Martial, in those trying years at Rome, thought yearningly of his native Bilbilis in Spain. But it is significant that with Peacham it is principally the *literary* associations:[50]

> I think the place that gave me first my birth,
> The *genius* had of epigram and mirth;
> There famous *Moore* did his Utopia wright
> And thence came *Heywoods* Epigrams to light.[51]

This nostalgia undoubtedly accounts for his urge, in the spirit of "whan that Aprille," to enjoy, after the winter of his discontent, the fresh air of spring.[52]

> So now this Spring my merry Muse and I
> Must walke the world abroad and take the aire,
> Who at our worke all Winter close did ly.

The point has already been made that Peacham was versatile. One of the professions he tried was teaching; but it did not satisfy him. In a turn of phrase that is quite characteristic of him he protests that, while the Wymomdham school at which he taught was "free," he, the master, "lost my libertie."[53] The whole profession, he finds to his consternation, is held in disesteem; and in his own experience he learns that it is "one of the most laborious callings in the World."[54] Tutoring was at times equally distasteful,[55] the parents being apt to blame the tutor for their offsprings' failures: "If hee falls in climbing a Dawes nest, his Master is in fault."[56] And his great peroration to his chapter "Of Schooles and Masters" is:[57] "For my part, I have done with that profession, having evermore found the world unthankfull, how industrious soever I have beene."

From the above it might be assumed that Peacham was a failure in teaching. Quite the opposite is true if we are to judge by the expressions of warm affection and respect in various epigrams. For instance, the relationship between him and his pupil Edward Chamberlain reminds us in some points of that between Milton and his friends Edward King and Charles Diodati:[58]

To my towardly and hopefull Scholer
Maister *Edward Chamberlaine* of *Barnham Broome:*

Ned, never looke againe those daies to see,
Thou livd'st, when thou appliedst thy booke with me,
What true affection bare we each to either,
How often walking in the fields together,
Have I in Latin giv'n the names to thee,
Of this wild Flower, that bent, this blossom'd tree,
This speckled Flie, that Hearb, this water rush,
This worme, or weed, the Bird on yonder bush?
How often when yee have beene ask'd a play,
With voices viols have we pass'd the day,
Now entertaining those weake aires of mine,
Anon the deepe delicious Transalpine,
Another while with pencill or with pen,
Have limnd or drawn our friends pourtraies, and then
Commixing many colours into one,
Have imitated some carnation,
Strange field-found flower, or a rare seene flie,
A curious land-schap or a clouded sky?
Then haply wearie of all these would goe
Unto that Poeme I have labourd so:
Thus past our leasureable hourers away;
And yee did learne even in the midst of play.

It is worth noting that the above lines were composed eighteen years before *Lycidas*.[59]

Gradually emerging through the epigrams were deep-seated convictions. From the beginning he showed his preference of the country over the city. This preference may stem partly from his experience as a youth and partly from his awareness of Martial. But he clearly would not have developed the idea in such detail if he had not had definite feelings about it. In "Ad Marcellum"[60] he strongly advises him, in the mood of Candide, to *cultiver votre jardin,* and he specifies a whole host of flowers, giving each its peculiar quality and emphasizing its symbolic meaning. Then he concludes:[61]

Lord wou [*sic*] would live within the Citie pent
Immured like a fish within a Well,

Where thou canst see the goodly firmament,
In some blind lane the space of scarce an ell?
I find the Citie to confound my senses
With loathed smels, with aire too thicke and muddy:
When this or that still drawes me to expenses,
And Cartes, and Coaches hinder me from study.
And leave those places where thou hast no place
Where cares vaine hopes and foule expences clog thee:
And where when gotten highest grace,
Foule envies eie at everie turne will dog thee.

Certainly the last two lines would have reminded us of Martial even if Peacham had not gone to the trouble of mentioning the Spaniard in the margin.[62] These same ideas are reenforced in *Minerva Britanna*[63] where he wants to be "remote from Citie, and the vulgar strife," to flee from the city's infection with its chaos and confusion. He wants rather a shady grove on the Thames above Richmond, or similar ones on the Severn or the Avon.

Peacham would readily have agreed with Professor F. J. Child who once said that there was nothing like keeping the open mind *except* the having two or three strong prejudices; they steady one so. Generally speaking, women did not stand high in his estimation.[64] This appears to be due to what may have been an unfortunate marriage. Because of an allusion in *The Truth of Our Times*[65] where he gives us the specific information, "I am not married; if I were, I should finde my wings clipt, and the collar too streight for my neck," scholars have set his unmarried status down as a fact.[65a] Malone rightly maintained that he *was* married. A simple explanation of the contradiction is that Peacham was separated; all we need do is change the tense and read "I *did* find my wings clipt." However that may be, he, like Dryden, seldom speaks respectfully of the married state. And like Milton he can speak with special verve because of personal experience; in an emblem headed "Matrimonium" he writes:

Who loveth best, to live in *Hymens* bandes,
And better likes, the carefull married state,
May here behold, how *Matrimonie* standes,
In woodden stocks, repenting him too late:
The servile yoake, his neck, and shoulder weares.
. . . .

The stockes doe shew, his want of libertie,
Not as he woont, to wander where he list:
The yoke's an ensigne of servilitie.[66]

And in an earlier emblem (119) he had spoken of four things that cause misery, "A Rod, the world, a Woman, Ages greife." He weeps for Dunmo who met his wife "in the great plague time" and has endured till now, "the thirtieth of her raigne."[67]

To mention another of his prejudices, Peacham clearly had no use for the French, and did not hesitate to ascribe the so-called French disease to its proper source:

Emson thou once in Dutch wouldst court a wench,
But to thy cost she answer'd thee in French.[68]

And, while satirizing a boastful world-traveler, he mentions one country which the fellow prefers not to talk about:

But since the pox some few daies since he got,
He never tels how *France* he found too hot.[69]

Peacham was sufficiently familiar with the *Greek Anthology* to know how wrong the French were in implying in their ridiculous *à la Grecque* expression that the Greek epigram had no sharp point.[70] Likewise, he would have discerned that the expression may have implied that the Greeks wrote no real epigrams because they were not obscene enough.

There were classes of society for which he had little or no sympathy. Always he distrusted the courtier; in fact, he appears to have regarded most of them as pests, calling on Judge Popham to rid the country of them.[71] In a later epigram he writes, "the Asse a Courtier on a time would be,"[72] implying that the two are interchangeable. But perhaps the best evidence comes in *Thestylis Atrata*.[72a] When all allowance has been made for the fulsome praise in many elegies, what Peacham says of the late Countess of Warwick has the note of sincerity; he admired her perhaps more than any lady he had known. It may be this sincerity that accounts in part for the distinct improvement in his handling of the decasyllabic couplet during the ten years that intervened between another elegy, *An Aprill Shower,* and *Thestylis Atrata.* At any rate, one of the high points is reached in the line, "The Court and Citie seld frequented she." And, putting his own words in the Countess' mouth he concludes,[73] "Adieu yee *Courts,* but *Cotes* of clay and stone."

As with most epigrammatists, Peacham's strictures were particularly severe on the hypocrites; and the worst were those in the church,[74] who were worse than Satan himself:

> The Hypocrite, that doth pretend in show,
> A feigned Zeale of Sanctitie within.
> . . . .
> Where *Lucifer* did openly rebell
> To God, these Traitors even within the Cell.

The accompanying emblem shows a churchman with the cross on a chain. The rich, especially the idle rich, fare no better.[75] In *Minerva Britanna*[76] he inveighs against avarice and, a little later,[77] scores idleness. How shall we busy ourselves this day, comes the question;[78] and the answer is just as prompt—play cards, go drink, or else go see a play. The interest in women is naturally associated, and Peacham illustrates this by what sounds like a contemporary anecdote;[79] "great *Bombos* heire" is so fascinated by watching the wenches play "at foote-ball" that his friends cannot dissuade him from staying over. Peacham has in mind "such heires as straight, their Patrimonie wast."[80] And, to illustrate further he makes adroit use of the Prodigal story:[81]

> Yet sweares, he never with the Hoggs did dine,
> That's true, for none durst trust him with their swine.

Peacham observed many an instance of some worthless scion spending himself into prison.[82] For jailbirds in general he cannot refrain from expressing his contempt;[83] to the man complaining that his name is not to be found in the church registry, Peacham advises him to look rather "in *Newgate* or the Poultry *Counter* booke."[84] With his strong tendency to moderation Peacham stands regularly against drunkenness and gourmandizing. He calls the former "loathsome."[85] An epigram in*Thalia's Banquet* illustrates another tendency of the genre, that of "cracking the whip" in the last line:

> *Methusus* asked me why I called him sot,
> I answere made, because he lov'd the pot,
> For while *Methusus* busie is with it,
> The foole I'me sure's as busie with his wit.[86]

There is a line of satirical portraits from "Sir Dolphin,"[87] who protests that no disgrace sullies his character but who is regularly found in alehouses in the company of tapsters, whores, and tinkers; from the man[88] who goes on his customary round of debauchery and chooses Sunday to lie abed and enjoy his hangover, "when he heares perhaps the sermon bel"; to "old *Sosibian*"[89] who can't make up his mind which he prefers, the "Porteis," which he keeps by his bed every night, or his "Alehouse Can," which is forever under his nose all day long. And with gourmandizing, Peacham is equally severe:

> Lodronio like a huge *Westphaly* swine,
> Lies close and never stirres without his doores,
> Feedes of the best, drinkes sack and claret wine,
> And at commandment hath his lease of whores,
> That *death* this hog would stick, the parrish pray,
> For to his hand hee's soundly sing'd they say.[90]

It is to be hoped that the name "Lodronio" covered a multitude of sins.

Certainly not too much should be made of Peacham's satire of the professions; from the beginning epigrammatists have satirized doctors and lawyers, poetasters and clergymen, travelers and schoolmasters. And it is only by reading between the lines that we can tell when he is being more than conventional. Martial[91] was particularly vicious with doctors, so vicious that we can but assume a personal experience. Peacham follows, telling with apparent relish the story[92] of a sick-to-death Spanish soldier who bequeathed his pistol to the doctor:

> This with your practice joyned, you may kill,
> Sir, all alive, and have the world at will.

Lawyers were no more fortunate. Of Tullus, who had changed his profession from tailor to lawyer, he writes,[93]

> So who before did cut but countrey freeze [frieze],
> Now cuts the Countrey in excessive fees.

Of the clergy, he writes:

> Tarquinius sweares that he had rather sterve,
> Then any living (God confound him) serve,
> We will beleeve him without further strife,
> Since yet he nere serv'd God in all his life.[94]

And a large part of *A Paradox in the Praise of a Dunce* is taken up with a bitter satire of ignorant and incompetent ministers.[94a] Of one obviously typical minister Peacham writes[95] that he believes his full Sunday duty to have been done if he merely reads "an Homily well."[96] In the same work[97] the author scores ineffective teachers: "Notable are the absurdities of Dunsticall Schoole-Masters." Here, in particular, Peacham knew whereof he spoke.

Walter Bagehot might have characterized Peacham, as he did Dickens, as a special correspondent for posterity; he had a keen and critical eye, as he walked about the streets of London, for the manners and fashions of his time. The natural place for him to exhibit this talent was, of course, in *The Truth of Our Times.* But there is many an instance in the epigrams. There is a quality of Thomas Dekker in his close observation. He cannot help laughing at Soranzo's absurdly big hat; but the fashion gives him a chance to reflect on the man's stupidity:

His head, the Earth's Globe fixed under it,
Whose Center is his wondrous little wit.[98]

He was enough of a true-born Englishman to deplore the apish imitation of foreign fashions. He is honestly shocked at the way women paint themselves, Flavia reminding him in her flagrant white and red of some street sign, "the Mercers maiden-hed;"[99] and he warns Gellia that she had better wear her mask in the sun lest her gross painting melt.[100] But his most apt comparison of all is with Trinity College, the college he knew best from undergraduate days:[101]

The faire *Dorinda* dressed *cap a pie*
In state, resembles *Cambridge Trinitie,*
Her, her all turret, and of wondrous cunning,
Her back-side broade, and front full faire in shew,
Onely her teeth stand like old *rotten Row.*[102]

And further he has well observed the loose ladies in their pretentious gilt coaches riding to rendezvous with "some sweet hart," having told their husbands they were going "to meete the nurse."[103] He cannot help noticing and commenting on the slow progress being made on St. Paul's tower:

Saint *Maries* steeple's up and ready soone,
But *Paules* 'tis thought will lie abed till noone.[104]

To another of London's famous landmarks he pays tribute:

> Constancie in the frost, faire bridge of London,
> Was a virtue in thee, else had we been undone.[105]

Of the thriving theatre Peacham seems to have been particularly impressed with the comic actor Tarlton. He speaks in *The Truth of Our Times*[106] of having seen him, "when I was a School-boy in *London*," acting the part of a prodigal, and goes into detail about his stage appearance "in a foule shirt without a band, and in a blew coat with one sleeve, his stockings out at the heeles, and his head full of straw and feathers." In *Thalia's Banquet*[107] he had already broached the subject:

> As *Tarlton* when his head was onely seene,
> The Tire-house doore and Tapistrie betweene,
> Set all the multitude in such a laughter,
> They could not hold for scarce an houre after,
> So (Sir) I set you (as I promis'd) forth,
> That all the world may wonder at your worth.

No one could saunter through the streets of London in those venturesome times without running into a host of people who had traveled to foreign shores. One rather elaborate sketch by Peacham lists the many sights a traveler only claims to have seen;[108] each of these sights was conventionally accepted as characteristic of the country described. The lying traveler appears also in an earlier epigram of *Thalia's Banquet*[109] with his tall tale of Russia's cold being so severe that men blow off their noses when they sneeze. And the "character" gets his final objectification in the two lines:

> For of his travels he hath told more lies,
> Then *Mandevile* could for his heart devise.[110]

Following Martial and anticipating Pope, Peacham naturally does not spare the pretenders in his own profession:

> I read thy booke *Vulturus* thou didst give mee,
> Twise over, walking under Arden wood,
> Which having throughly perus'd, beleeve me,
> Save thy Epistle ther was nothing good.[111]

Such lines have the same blistering effect as those near the beginning of *The Epistle to Dr. Arbuthnot.*

PEACHAM AND THE EPIGRAM: MANNER

The previous chapter dealt primarily with the *matter* of Peacham's epigrams; this chapter will deal mostly with the *manner*.

First, something should be said about his attitude towards poetry in general and his own poetry in particular. What he thought the objectives of poetry should be is well expressed in his advice to a fellow poet in *The More the Merrier:*[1]

> See that thou nothing write in private hate,
> Or which may touch Religion, or the state,
> Use honest [decent] tearmes, and loath lewd bawdry,
> Well maist thou thrive, then, with thy Poesie.

But already in his dedication[2] to the same work he had pointed out the limitations of his own verse and the conceivable misinterpretations that might be set on it: "Some grave Divine will doubt of my soundnes in religion, the polititian that I meddle with the state, the Lawyer that I inveigh at him, Ladies and Gentlewomen, that I taxe onely their pride and vanitie." The answer to such hypothetical charges is given in a considerably later work, *Thalia's Banquet:*[3]

> For as my mind is merry, honest, free
> It's image, so my veine and verses bee.

At the same time it is interesting to note the audience he thinks he is addressing; Thalia speaks and bids the following to participate in her banquet:[4]

> From the Colledge and the Hall,
> Welcome Academicks all,

Brittaines Magazins of Wit,
Innes of Court repaire to it
And some Courtiers ye that be
The Mirrour of faire courtesie,
Citizens ye that were made
As well for learning as for trade,
Come brave spirits of the Realme,
Unshaded of the Academe
That in the Countrey there and here,
Like starres in midst of Clouds appeare.
. . . .
And brave Souldiers take a truce,
A while to revell with his Muse,
Since our Author hath borne Armes too,[5]
He cannot chuse but welcome you:
Come faire Ladyes ye that will,
Heere is nought obscure or ill,
And your maids Attendants, some
Witty wenches let them come.

The multifariousness of the readers summoned would almost indicate that Peacham was lending a hand to the stationer in the book's sale! He confirms his purpose when at the conclusion to the same work[6] he claims to have written "no dull conceite, no jest that's poore and leane."

Like most poets, Milton included, Peacham looks forward to writing a more serious type of poetry:[7]

Bid now my Muse, thy lighter taske adieu,
As shaken blossome of a better fruite,
And with *Urania* thy Creator view,
To sing of him, or evermore be mute.

In a similar vein Milton was to write some fifteen years later:

Yet I had rather if I were to chuse,
Thy service in some graver subject use,
Such as may make thee search thy coffers round,
Before thou cloath my fancy in fit sound:
Such where the deep transported mind may soare
Above the wheeling poles, and at Heav'ns dore
Look in.

He went on to address Urania, the "Heav'nlie borne," at the opening of Book VII of *Paradise Lost.* A further analogy might be drawn between Milton's asking his reader's forbearance when he comes

> To pluck your Berries harsh and crude,
> And with forc'd fingers rude,
> Shatter your leaves before the mellowing year, . . .

and Peacham's similar mood in *Thalia's Banquet:*[8]

> Reader, if that thy curious eye will needes
> Dwel on a while these rude and ranker weedes,
> Take leave; and ere a while this Muse of ours
> Shal bring thee lapfuls of her choisest flowers.

Like most poets Peacham also had periods of profound discouragement when he felt like abandoning poetry altogether; G. S. Gordon says[9] that this was clearly his mood after *Thalia's Banquet.* He was then forty-two, regarded in the seventeenth century as a reasonably advanced age. Even earlier he had had the sense of ebbing power:[10]

> My dying Muse doth like a taper wast,
> Tread out her snuffe, and then the worst is past.

It is incredible that so good a classical scholar should not be familiar with the *Greek Anthology,*[11] and one has the feeling often that he is following tradition. Though there was much in Peacham's life to make him especially value independence and deplore servility, he must have been aware of the Alexandrian Palladas, with whom he had so much in common; Palladas[12] declared that though he was poor, he had freedom as his housemate and he took a satisfaction in turning his back on wealth that insulted poverty. Further, Palladas,[13] like Peacham, expressed well the miseries of the schoolmaster. It is easy to carry such analogies too far. Clearly Peacham knew how the Greeks stressed the simple life, the golden mean, how they contended that money was the root of all evil,[14] how they assailed hypocrites and pretenders. Yet there is something firsthand in most of Peacham's allusions to these very matters. Theognis[15] may have written, "I neither wish nor pray for wealth; my prayer is for a small subsistence, free from care." But when Peacham commends the simple life, he writes as if the Greek had never existed; he convinces the reader that such sentiments come from the heart,[16] as they undoubtedly do.

Much the same may be said for Peacham's relation with Martial. Certainly he was familiar with the Roman's great popularity during the Renaissance and with the English epigrammatists who followed him. But there is hardly a place where he is said to have imitated Martial that the manner or matter does not derive naturally from his own ideas. Martial[17] protests that his rule is "to spare the person, to denounce the vice"; in *The More the Merrier*[18] Peacham avoids "inveighing at any mans private person." The main difference here is that when Peacham unsheathes his satirical dagger it is apt, as he says,[19] "to proove but a woodden one." Both poets declare that epigrams occupy a modest position on the poetic scale;[20] but almost from the beginning the genre's humble status was recognized. In fact, each poet excuses his free language with the rhetorical query, "What can you expect from the epigram?"[21] Peacham follows Martial in voting for the simple life, in preferring the country to the city,[21a] as many poets do. This one aspect seems to draw the two poets singularly close together. Both had an almost fanatic nostalgia.[21b] All through the long, exhausting years in the confusion of Rome, Martial yearned for his native Bilbilis. And whenever he thinks of it, he proudly thinks that he may have put it on the map. After telling how other poets have made their birthplaces famous, he concludes, "Our Bilbilis will be proud of you, Licinianus, nor will be altogether silent concerning me."[22] In the same way Peacham shows undisguised pride in his own North Mimms:[23]

> Who would not sweare the Towne that gave me birth,
> Her *Genius* had infus'de of harmles mirth,
> Where first devised were at idle times,
> *Sir Thomas Moores,* old *Heywoods,* and my rimes.

In other ways the similarity between the two poets is apt to have been coincidental. Both had a low opinion of women,[24] but Peacham had his personal reasons which made him go well beyond merely arraigning the sex for painting their faces. Before he is through, he has accused women of talking too much, of trying to manage everything, of allowing no peace, of being lazy, and of being inveterate liars.[25] If Martial spends many a line complaining that he lacks sesterces, that he has not a farthing in the house, and that he is compelled to live in a garret,[26] Peacham[27] protests that his purse is chronically purged. The *Worth of a Penny: or a Caution to Keep Money* is, up to a point, Peacham's complaint to his purse. The corollary with both poets is that they detest the rich, or pretend to. The Roman is bitter; if you want to get rich, he tells Bithynicus, become a panderer to vice.[28] It is no accident that the Prodigal acts as a theme in *Minerva Britanna*. The result is that both inveigh against talent's not being rewarded.[29] Here too Martial[30] is especially bitter; while Scorpus, "a winner of the race," gets fifteen bags of gleaming gold in an hour, he, the poet, earns a paltry hundred farthings in a whole day. Finally, both poets use their epigrams to voice their sharp criticism of poetasters. To Cosconius, who asserted that Martial's epigrams were too long, the latter replied that Cosconius' very distichs were too long.[30a] In *Thalia's Banquet*, "Upon Dare an upstart Poet,"[31] Peacham has some similarly barbed lines.

A word should be said about where Peacham did *not* follow the classical epigram; sometimes a poet's basic qualities can be discerned in what he chose to omit. From Simomides down, Greek poetry is full of eloquent laments for those drowned at sea.[32] It has been said that in sixteenth- and seventeenth-century England the family that did not have a relative or friend who had so perished was the great exception. It may be that Peacham was among those exceptions; the fact remains that no such lament appears in his poetry.[33] Perhaps it is hardly worth noting that the element of love is absent from his epigrams. Though the selections from Meleager are about four-fifths amatory,[34] there are long periods represented by the *Greek Anthology* during which love played only a minor role.[35] Certainly Peacham knew that the element seldom appeared in Martial, and he was aware, also, that Ben Jonson had little of it.[36] He may have omitted it because of personal experience. He never mentioned making the most of love while it lasts; he left that to Marvell. Perhaps, on the contrary, "love" for him had lasted too long.[37]

Something of the same may be said for his failure to make more use of nature. Here again the Greek *Anthology* has stretches where little is made of it. Professor Mackail argues that in the classical period, for example, nature is incidental. It really does not become prominent until the Alexandrian period. Where Peacham does use nature, he usually makes it subservient; in the "flowers" passage of *The More the Merrier*[38] he is merely trying to show his preference for the simple life.

What Peacham wrote of emblem literature (in English) may be extended in part to include his attitude towards English epigrams:[39] "I know not an *Englishman* in our age, that hath published any worke of this kind . . . except the collections of Master *Whitney,* and the translations of some one or two else beside."[40] It is quite possible that he thought of himself as something of an innovator in the native epigram. We must keep in mind that *The More the Merrier* antedated Jonson's epigrams by eight years. And clearly Peacham agreed with that poet in his low opinion of English epigrams. There is little in Turberville's *Epitaphes, Epigrams* (1567), Kendall's *Flowers* (1577), Guilpin's *Skialetheia* (1598), Bastard's *Chrestoleros* (1598), or Thynne's *Emblems and Epigrams* (1600), to make us think that *The More the Merrier* would have been essentially different if those collections had never existed. If Peacham did put some value on Heywood's work, it was more because that gentleman hailed from his home town. As for the rest, with the exception of very few, such as Sir John Davies, "the English Martial," Peacham recognized that for the most part their poetry was what Professor Raleigh unjustly called Warner's verse, "an accompaniment to stocking-weaving."[41]

It has been implied above that there was an extraordinary diversity about Peacham's epigrams; yet it can be said that there were certain tendencies which he characteristically emphasized. For example, he insisted that his concern was with faults, not individuals. In his dedication "To M.H.C." in *The More the Merrier* he says his satire is not directed "at any mans private person,"[42] and a few pages later in "To the Reader" he repeats this point, contending that it is not natural for him to keep "hate in my heart."[43] How much this was on his mind is shown by a distich in *Thalia's Banquet:*[44]

> Beleeve *Severus,* that in these my rimes
> I taske no person, but the common crimes.

Of course, not too much should be made of his claim; when Peacham refers to a "high-fee'd" lawyer under the Latin name of Tullus,[45] one has the uncomfortable feeling that contemporaries might know who was being referred to. Martial had done exactly the same when, with tongue in cheek, he said that, however closely pressed, he would never reveal the identity of his "Postumus."[46]

Like Wordsworth, any poet reserves the right to do what he says he will not do. In *Thalia's Banquet*[47] Peacham states:

> My banquet is prepar'd for *Wit,*[48]
> Not *Folly* dare to touch a bit.

In whatever sense he was using the word, Peacham was quite capable of relishing his own wit. While he was working in a monastery library in Shertogen Bosch in Brabant,[49] one of the friars wrote a Latin distich in Peacham's Greek Testament, "while I was busy perusing some bookes." The distich reflected humorously on England. Peacham retaliated, chuckling as he did so: "His back being turn'd, I left this behind me, in the first printed page of a faire *Arias Montanus* bible, to requite him." What he left, again in a good-humored vein, was a Latin poem reflecting on Holland.

If he protested that folly was not his concern, he had proved the contrary in *The More the Merrier*.[50] There he explicitly says, "In briefe the world of folly I upbraid." And as if to drive the point home he repeats,[51] "I doe but note the follies of our age." On the other hand, twelve years intervened between *The More the Merrier* (1608) and *Thalia's Banquet* (1620), and in that amount of time, any man is justified in changing his emphasis.

While looking for the underlying tones of Peacham's poetry, we should note his deep respect for learning and his profound regret that it was held in such disesteem by his contemporaries.[51a] Emblem 26 of *Minerva Britanna* is an eloquent tribute to learning, and Peacham's high admiration for Maurice, landgrave of Hessia, is due to that "most noble" Prince's being possessed of "admirable knowledge in all learning and the languages."[52]

Miss Pitman's conjecture[53] that he may have taken holy orders would account in part for the strong moralizing note that runs through much of Peacham's poetry. This is especially obvious in *Minerva Britanna* where, though the substance is often secondhand, the emphasis given is clearly Peacham's; his deepest convictions emerge from the conclusions he reaches. When, for instance, he is inveighing against the age for its shameful neglect of the lutenist John Dowland, he writes:[54]

> Ingratefull times and worthles age of ours,
> That let's us pine when it hath cropt our flowers.

Such a distich reveals not merely his general disillusionment, but specifically his complaint against neglect of the arts. In the next emblem[55] he stresses a thought which is similarly deep-rooted:

> Great Lordes, and Ladies, turne your cost and art
> From bodies pride, t'enritch your better part.

Here also two persuasions are expressed: his resentment against the Court's snobbishness and his insistence on cultivating the mind. Often such general inferences come at the poem's end; the following[56] has all the ring of Pope, or of Raphael's advice to Adam in the eighth book[57] of *Paradise Lost:*

> Be wise in what the word doth plainely teach,
> But meddle not with thinges above thy reach.

Much like Herbert's *Church Porch, Minerva Britanna* presents us with a series of moral precepts, such as "Beware a lavish tongue,"[58] and the slow starter often goes farther.[59] Several times he appears to be lecturing to himself:[60]

> Then some one calling choose, whence good may growe,
> And let the rest, as needelesse branches goe.

It is well known that Peacham tried his hand at many vocations.[61] Following his usual theme of moderation, he warns against all work and no play in language that is strikingly similar to Charles Diodati's while lecturing Milton:[62]

> Let idle fits refresh thy daylie paine,
> And with some Labour exercise thy rest,
> For overmuch of either, duls the spright,
> And robs our life, of comfort and delight.

Finally, in the last emblem[63] he insists that life regularly deceives with false promises, though, in the nature of the genre, he quotes his various authorities for such a conclusion.

With this strong tendency to moralize, it is hardly surprising to find Peacham asserting that he does not indulge in the epigram's indecency. He well knew the genre's reputation.[64] Martial[65] had defended his own liberties by citing the case of Catullus. He goes on[66] to concede that "no page of mine is without freedoms of language." Peacham knew, also, that the tendency in English epigrams had been a cleansing one. Guilpin[67] indicated the general attitude:

> Excuse me (Reader) though I now and than,
> In some light lines doe shew my selfe a man,
> Nor be so sowre, some wanton words to blame,
> They are the language of an Epigrame.

In his odd language Thomas Bastard[68] claimed that he had taught epigrams to speak chastely; and Timothy Kendall,[69] in like manner, protests "as well out of *Martial* as the rest, I have left the lewde, I have chosen the chaste."

Frequently, Peacham declares his purpose to minimize obscenity. The very title of *Thalia's Banquet* contains the promise of "inoffensive mirth." And earlier in *The More the Merrier*,[70] he meant exactly the same when he insisted that "honest mirth" never comes out of season. He proceeds to explain his point: "Concerning unsavorie lewdnesse (which many of our *Epigrammatists* so much affect) I have esteemed it fitter for Pickhatch." All such he will leave to "foule mouth'd *Aretine*."[71] On the other hand, Peacham gives the impression that he is allowing himself some leeway when in the same passage of *The More the Merrier* he hopes that his epigrams are not "over luscious for obscenitie"; whereupon, he significantly quotes four lines from Martial. This hedging is then repeated in one of the epigrams,[72] where he uses characteristically blunt language:

> Be not agreeved my humorous lines affoord
> Of looser language heere and there a word,
> Who undertakes to sweepe a common sincke,
> I cannot blame him though his besome stincke.

This is something of an understatement; there are passages which would hardly serve as required reading in a nunnery. For example:[73]

> Mildred my Ladie Too-goods chambermaid,
> Hath now her wages by her Maister paid,
> Not quarterly, but duely once a yeare,
> And in a purse as bigge as she can beare.

Another example is the epigram[74] about the footman Nocturnus (well named) who was accustomed to jog along beside his master's gelding:

> He [the master] dead, his Mistris lik'd so well his pace,
> He now at ease doth in the saddle ride.

Peacham must have been aware of the satire in the Greek Anthology, introduced to a large extent by Lucian and Lucilius. In the same way he knew the vein running through the Latin epigrams of More[75] and of John Owen (Audoenus), the Welshman, the latter's case being notorious because his little poem "S. Peter at Rome" succeeded in putting his volume on the Index. There was, further, some tendency of Peacham's time that lent itself to satire; as he writes in the Epistle Dedicatory to *Coach and Sedan,*[76] "Wee live in that Age, wherein Difficule est Satyram non scribere." But our poet is quite right in saying that his satire normally lacks sharpness or bitterness:[77] "I will never draw my dagger, till I be stricken: and if I chance to unsheath it, they need not feare me, since it is likely to proove but a woodden one," a figure he could have lifted from Sir John Harington[78] who wrote:

> What should I wish Itis for this abuse,
> But to his leaden sword, a woodden dagger.

Thus, when Peacham says,[79] "as for Satyrick inveighing at any mans private person, (a kind of writing which of late seemes to have beene very familiar among our Poets and Players to their cost) my reader is to seeke it else where," we cannot but agree with his self-criticism. Bishop Hall would probably have called his satires "toothless," a term that would apply more appropriately to Peacham's than to his own.

In the satirical category belongs also the so-called caricature epigram. This is one place where Peacham's contributions appear "derived," perhaps because it was not his usual habit to make fun of his contemporaries. He does have several epigrams on the human feature so caricatured in our comic valentine, the nose. It is significant that he gives one[80] epigram the unrevealing title of "Ad Nasonem." Another[81] has the person, if there is any, masquerading under a bizarre name; having gone into great detail about a monstrous jewel that contained almost every flamboyant color in the spectrum, he concludes,

> I never saw this wonder, but suppose,
> It much resembled *Oenopolio's* nose.

It is much more likely that Peacham was actively aware of how the nose came in for its ribbing in classical times. After all, it is not surprising that the "Roman" nose should have received attention from the Latins. Ammianus is one *inter alia.*[81a]

As with almost everything else in Peacham, there are exceptions to his avoiding the satirical approach. He knew Martial's brilliant sallies in this area in spite of the Roman's disclaimer[82] that "my page injures not even those whom it justly hates." The man that Martial cannot abide above all others is the would-be poet who pesters him with his own poor verses. Here Peacham agrees, probably out of his own bitter experience.[82a]

Though it is true that Peacham interested himself in so many things that he did not have time to revise as he should, we know that he did emphasize the importance of revision. In lines that form a bridge between Horace and Pope he offers the following advice:[83]

> What ere thou writ'st, see carefully the same,
> Thou oft peruse, and after pause, and stay;
> Mend what's amisse, with *Argus* hundred eies.

As a result of his own revising, he has many an epigram that is neatly turned. Though here again he may lay claim to originality, one has the feeling that Martial's brilliant technique is in the back of his mind. The Latin poet had clearly cultivated the art of reserving his point to the last line, which clinched the whole thought. For instance, when he wishes[84] to pay high tribute to the emperor, he goes into considerable detail about a resplendent new palace, then concludes by saying that though "its pinnacle touches the stars" [it] "is less than its lord." Or he chides Polycharmus for often pretending to be ill in order to get presents and bids him for heaven's sake to make the next his last[85] illness. Peacham has dozens of such epigrams. He will, for example, make adroit use of Thomas Tusser's well-known husbandry:[86]

> *Tusser* they tell me when thou wert a live,
> Thou teaching thrift thy selfe couldst never thrive,
> So like whetstone many men are woont,
> To sharpen others when them selves are blunt.

He can glance at the deplorable simony of his day:[87]

> Sir *Harpax* when a Benefice doth fall,
> Enquires about for him that will give most.
> . . . .
> Hence *Harpax* sweares, among his other shifts,
> He none preferres but men of *passing gifts*.

Or he will reflect upon the morals of the age: he notes that Milla's maid has so well practiced Aristotelian communicativeness that she has "growne hereby as big as she can go."[88] In the same way he advises the expectant father, who is busy exploring his books in order to cast his baby's future, to look rather backwards, "and learne for certaine who had beene the father." His tendency to be skeptical of women can be observed in an epigram that carefully reserves its point till the final line:[89]

> Anna protestes she never kist but once,
> Or ever for a husband car'd but once,
> She never falsified her word but once
> Or fell out with her dearest friend but once,
> Or ever tooke a Cup too much but once,
> Or plaid at Cardes all Sermons while but once,
> I'le adde once more unto her *Onely* stile,
> She never lied but once, that's all this while.

Though Peacham was seldom condescending to foreign nations,[90] he does expose the Dutchman's notorious drunkenness.[91] While traveling in Holland he had noticed how people were in the habit of inscribing their favorite beers on the walls of their houses:

> Yet though the beere of sundry natures be,
> In their being drunke no difference did I see.

His ability to turn a nice compliment is shown in his tribute[92] to Alice Apsley, "daughter to the virtuous Lady the L. Apsley":

> As Virgins, when with dainty fingers weave
> Their girlands, place the fairest flowers in view,
> So heere I set your beauty by your leave,
> To grace my booke (faire maide) and honor you.

He can do the same[93] for his "very worthy and honest friend Maister *Robert Constable of Hingham*":

> As pretious wares we see are often wrapt
> In papers small, so fares it with me now,
> Who in these leaves my dearest love have lapt
> And sent it as a token unto you,
> Who of a *Constable* deserves to be
> A Justice for your braine and honestie.

Peacham would hardly belong to the seventeenth century if he did not indulge occasionally in such puns. The experience of Sir Thomas Browne was enough evidence to prove the importance of Leyden as a center for medical studies, and Peacham[94] seizes on the name to make his pun:

Sartor at *Leyden* hath commenc'd, they say,
And come a leaden Doctor thence away.

The pun itself is somewhat leaden; but then many puns are.

To implement his poetry Peacham resorted naturally to the storehouses of Elizabethan imagery. By 1600, for example, mythology had been used so often that it was difficult even for a Shakespeare to breathe new life into it. Peacham did at least as well as most poets in adapting the lore to his purposes:[95]

As then the Skie was calme and faire,
The Windes did cease, and Cloudes were fled,
Aurora scattered *Phoebus* haire,
New risen from her Rosie bed:
At whose approach the Harlot[96] strew,
Both meade, and mountaine, with her flowers:
While *Zephyre* sweetest odours threw,
About the feildes, and leavie bowers.

Or he can couch his advice to the lovelorn Ann Dudley by telling her that to avoid "*Cupids* might" she must imitate Diana and go hunting.[97]

In the same way Peacham makes full use of the historical anecdote. Still under the spell of the Renaissance, he appears to think that there is something magical about examples from the Ancients. While driving home the lesson of reticence, he cites the case of Solon who cut out his own tongue.[98] He can use, with some skill, the famous anecdote about Tiberius and the beggar. With his great yearning for the quiet life, Peacham naturally turns to the story of Augustus' requesting the bed of the dead man who had managed to sleep peacefully while alive.[99]

One of Peacham's chief interests while he was a student at Cambridge was history,[100] and it is natural, therefore, that his own country should play its part. In *Minerva Britanna*[101] he refers to Richmond's having overcome Richard "at that fatall feild of *Bosworth*"; in the same work[102] he glorifies British kings, and heroes "who serv'd *Eliza* in her raigne." Among those so glorified is the great explorer, Sir Hugh Willoughby. This must have been one of Peacham's special interests because in *Thestylis Atrata*[103] he emphasizes "Captaine John Smith . . . who . . . made a great discoverie in the North parts of *America*"; and just below, he refers to "wisest

Burghley, Atlas of our State."[104] He did not hesitate to use more earthy anecdotes such as the one told of the Emperor Charles V; "all a winters rainy night," Charles, hard pursued by *"Hessens* Lantgrave *Maurice,"* came by chance upon the simple hut of a Dutch boor of whom he asked the time of night; and the churl managed in the dark to tell the hour exactly by a regular nightly habit of his.[105]

To these historical anecdotes Peacham added ones from his own contemporary London, the sort of thing that was doubtless recorded in the black-letter literature of the day. The "silent highway" [of the Thames] naturally plays its part in this tradition:[106]

A Justice walking ore the frozen Thames,
The Ice about him round began to cracke,
He said to's man heere is some danger James,
I prethe helpe me over on thy backe.

Another winter incident is recorded[107] of "capring *Dicke*" whose head was "serv'd but a slippery trick." There is, also, the graphic picture of the dignified gentleman[108] who has his wig blown off as he rides along. There is such an abundance of circumstantial detail about these stories that Peacham accepts it as a challenge to see how much he can pack into his poetry. This is certainly true of the epigram[109] about Nasuto who, after hearing it said in table talk that "well taken *Discords*" could please the ear, concluded that, if such were accepted as criterion, he "should soone be sent for to the Archdukes quire." It is also true of the later epigram[110] in which the ingenious knight defers paying his debt for fourteen years, the period given his creditor-apprentice so that he might practice fencing before the knight will condescend to duel with him.

One has only to read Browne's *Pseudodoxia Epidemica* to realize the great importance natural history enjoyed in Peacham's century.[111] It is, therefore, not at all surprising that he should have resorted to it so often for his imagery. *Minerva Britanna* is full of such imagery. In emblem 89, for example, he makes the most of the silkworm. And in emblem 94 while drumming on one of his favorite subjects, the importance of maintaining one's independence, he uses an analogy with the falcon which, like Peacham, would prefer to be free,

Then [than] eate some caterpillar's envied bread,
Or at anothers curtesie be fed.

The gobbling crocodile is used to represent man's enemy[112]

> Who evermore lies watching, to devoure
> Our *Hopes* encrease.

As for the notorious viper,[113] just as her ungrateful offspring gnaws through her belly to "bring her to her end," so does "Beastly lust" operate on mankind. I do not wish to give the impression that Peacham presented an exceptional amount of natural history lore; in terms of seventeenth-century poetry, his presentation was about average.[114]

Our poet must have felt that references to famous people, past and present, would lend a certain substance to his poetry; it appears that a larger-than-usual quota of such names occurs throughout his verses. Once more Peacham was quite aware that this was something of a tradition in the epigram. Among others, the list includes Drayton, Selden, More, John Heywood, Beza, Erasmus, Sidney, Jonson, Surrey, Bacon, as well as the two great musicians, William Byrd and John Dowland. In his poem "To Maister Michael Drayton"[115] he deplores the low state of poetry in his time and asks when such men as Surrey and "our *Phoenix Sydney*" are going to reappear. He harps again on the lack of patrons, saying that most do not understand or appreciate real poetry. He returns to Sidney in *Minerva Britanna*[116] when he is regretting the vanished age of great Elizabeth, and, as an example, underscores in the margin the name of Sir Philip. In the distich "To Mr. Ben Johnson"[117] he pays that gentleman a nice compliment through the very shortness of the tribute:

> Since more cannot be added to thy Fame,
> Enough tis onely to expresse thy Name.

More and Heywood, as fellow townsmen, would naturally be mentioned, though it is significant that he brings them prominently into both *Thalia's Banquet*[118] and *The More the Merrier*.[119] Further, in "To the Reader"[120] Peacham asserts that better men than he have written satire, among them "learned sir *Thomas Moore*."[121] He has an emblem in *Minerva Britanna*[122] addressed "To the most judicious, and learned, Sir FRANCIS BACON, Knight." He praises a contemporary who, in light of his standing in his own time, has had far too little attention, John Selden. The sixth epigram in *Thalia's Banquet* is "To Mr. I. Selden of the Inner Temple."[123] In this epigram Peacham says that just as a novice painter, to encourage business, will put the picture of some famous statesman in his shop-window in the Strand, so he will place Selden's mighty name where it will encourage the reader to continue. In a passage of *The More the Merrier*[124] he mentions the French theologian Theodore Beza and the "late Erasmus." And finally, because of his great love of music,[125] he pays tribute[126] "To Maister *William Bird,* the glory of our Nation for Musique," and in "To Maister Doctor *Dowland,*"[127] he wrote:

> Your word, *Hinc illae lachrimae,* beneath,
> A *Venice* Lute within a laurell wreath.

He had already referred to Dowland in *Minerva Britanna,*[128] "Ad amicum suum Johannem Doulandum Musices peritissimum." He shows his closeness to this musician in the course of praising a German[129] noted for his "learning in all artes" including music: "Mr. Douland hath many times shewed me 10 or 12 severall sets of Songes for his [the German's] Chappel of his owne composing."

It is clear that Peacham had unusual capacity for friendship. This is not to say that he was an Izaak Walton, to whom all doors were open. But there are too many addresses to "kind friends" to leave us in doubt about his numerous friendships. As in many other ways, he was also like Martial in sending his verses to friends, to "my very worthy and honest friend" Robert Constable, for instance,

> Who in these leaves my dearest love have lapt
> And sent it as a token unto you.[130]

He does the same with another: "Dearest of frendes, accept this small device."[131] In the same work[132] he addresses an emblem "To my worshipfull and kind frend Mr. William Stallenge, searcher of the Port of London, and first Author of making Silke in our Land." *Thalia's Banquet* is sprinkled with such references. He especially admired Sir John Heveningham[133] for his honesty, a quality Peacham is constantly emphasizing. He addresses a later epigram[134] to "my Kind friend Captaine *Henry Lucy,* the Paragon of Chivalry"; and in a still later one[135] he thanks his host for his gracious hospitality. He pays tribute[136] also "To my kind and learned friend Maister *Owen Hughes* of *Remerstone*" as well as to[137] "the onely favourer of the Muse . . . Maister *Dru Drurie* of *Riddlesworth*." Sir John Ogle was "my especiall friend, with whom I lived in Utrecht."[138] He was an intimate friend of the famous mathematician and hydrographer, Edward Wright; and he also knew Ben Jonson's "friend," Inigo Jones quite well. In other words, there is ample evidence, even when we allow for conventional tributes, to prove that Peacham's friendships were warm and lasting.

THE ELEGY

As with the epigram, it will also be necessary to examine the elegy by considering the nature of the genre as it was practiced in the period immediately before Peacham's.[1] The first point to note regarding the Elizabethans[2] is the comparative paucity of their funeral elegies. Here we must carefully distinguish the funeral from the pastoral elegy[3] and so disregard Spenser's tribute to Sidney in "Astrophel,"[4] his memorial to Arthur Gorges' wife in "Daphnaida," and his November Eclogue in which he pays tribute to the "altogether unknowne" lady. It is true that Sidney was so honored, though it is significant that Bryskett's contribution is entitled "A Pastorall Aeglogue upon the Death of Sir Phillip Sidney, Knight," and Drayton's references in the Fourth Eclogue of *The Shepheards Garland* (1593) to "Elphin" the "God of Poesie" and "immortall mirror of all Poesie," are cast in the traditional pastoral form. Herbert of Cherbury's "Epitaph"[5] belongs to the next century. Still more significant is the fact that comparatively few elegies appear to have been written even on Elizabeth herself or at least are not extant. Sylvester[6] has a short epitaph on the Queen, and John Lane[7] has his "Elegie on the Death of Queen Elizabeth" (1603). Giles Fletcher[8] has a callow "Canto upon the Death of Eliza," and his brother,[9] Phineas, combines his tribute to Elizabeth with his joy on the accession of James. John Fenton's "Sorrowfull Epitaph"[10] is but twenty lines in length. Thus, Chettle is the exception; *Englands Mourning Garment: Worne here by plaine Shepheardes; in memorie of their sacred Mistresse, Elizabeth*"[11] is obviously in the pastoral elegiac tradition,[12] the interlocutors being those old standbys Thenot and Collin. The work is largely prose with a little poetry scattered in. And it has an historical bias, together with an eye-witness account of the funeral details.

The reason for its importance today is Chettle's scolding of his contemporary poets for not penning their tributes to the great Queen, among them probably Daniel, Drayton, Warner, and Shakespeare. The prose is followed by "The Funeral Song between Collin and Thenot, Dryope and Chloris, upon the Death of the sacred Virgin Elizabeth." All told, "Englands Mourning Garment" occupies eighteen pages in the 1745 edition of *Harleian Miscellany*.[13]

As we move on further into the seventeenth century, we should observe the chief characteristics which elegies developed. John Draper's summary[14] of the Jacobean and Caroline periods will be sufficient though it should be remembered that Draper is avowedly preoccupied with the funereal mortuary aspect:

> Of the pieces called elegies, many are Classical love-poems; and, even in those that were occasioned by death, this occasion is commonly passed over, so that the writer may laud and magnify the subject's good deeds or indulge in casuistical discussion of immortality and like theological matter: realistic, funeral descriptions are brief and rare. About a score of elegies contain mortuary passages, most of them very short; and these may be looked upon as forerunners of the *genre*. Perhaps the first in time, and one of the most dubious as an example, is William Browne's elegy on Prince Henry (d. 1612). It is the nearest approach of the School of Spenser to the mortuary form; and its one mortuary touch, the "Labyrinth of Woe," is a highly metaphoric description of the mourners' desolation. The Schools of Jonson and of Donne, which reached their prime later in the century, have more to offer. Donne's *Obsequies on the Lord Harrington* (1614), in which the author imagines himself beside the grave "at night," furnishes a nearer approximation. Herbert's elegy *Upon the Death of a Gentleman* is too largely composed of the wise saws and pious truisms of morality and too little of concrete description. A better example is Jonson's poem *On the Death of Lady Jane Pawlet* (1631) with its ghost, its yew-tree, and its forced, exclamatory style.

The two characteristics that at once impress us are the conventional nature of these elegies and the fact that nearly all of them are written on or for people of high birth who are potential patrons. If Dr. Johnson had taken the trouble to read the hundreds of examples of conventional poems, he might not have written as he did of

"Lycidas." It may be that the all-too-familiar trappings of the pastoral genre predetermined, in part, the nature of the other kind. Draper[15] quite properly calls our attention to the fact that in early seventeenth-century elegies, the death of the individual is glossed over,[16] and Hanford[17] characterizes Milton's effusions as "impersonal academic exercises." We can choose our examples almost at random. William Browne has a whole series of epitaphs[18] in which he plays linguistic tricks such as,[19]

> A horrid ill her kisses bit away,
> And gave her almost lipless to the clay.

Some of them even have the swing of Cavalier lyrics. The only one that shows any feeling is, significantly, the one "On His Wife."[20] Quarles[21] has a rather typical list of subjects: Sir Julius Caesar, "My Deare Brother," Sir Edmond Wheeler, "my honoured Friend, Dr. Wilson," "Mildreiados, Mildred La. Luckyn," Sir Robert Quarles, Sir John Wolstenholme, and the famous sisters "Countess of Cleaveland and Mistresse Cicily Killegrue." In these he also plays poetic tricks. For instance, there is "An Alphabet of Funeral Elegies" on Dr. Ailmer, "Arch-deacon of London,"[22] the *raison d'être* of the title proceeding from the fact that each elegy starts with a successive letter of the alphabet. John Davies of Hereford in "Muses Teares" also indulges in word-play.[23] All of the preceding examples Dr. Johnson could more justly accuse of lacking feeling. Crashaw[24] wrote several elegies (or epitaphs) on a man he called "Mr. Herrys," a Fellow of Pembroke Hall. But the man's true image never comes through:

> Yet in this Ground his pretious Root
> Still lives, which when weake Time shall be pour'd out
> Into Eternity, and circular joyes
> Dance in an endlesse round, againe shall rise
> The faire son of an ever-youthfull Spring,
> To be a shade for Angels while they sing.

It should be said that this is about what we might expect from Crashaw. His "Epitaph Upon Doctor Brooke"[25] consists in its entirety of a pun on Brooke's name. Drayton[26] writes of an unidentified Eleanor Fallowfield, giving us little or no sense that the woman was ever flesh and blood. Drummond[27] similarly conveys no feeling for Lady Jane Maitland, and little more for "his Much Loving and Beloved Master, Mr. John Ray."[28] Indeed, perhaps the pun on Ray's name, "Bright Ray of learning," was too much to resist. Wallerstein's observation that Joseph Beaumont's elegy on Edward King is dominated by rationalism to the exclusion of personal feeling[29] is well taken. And Cleveland's poem,[30] also on King, is marred by elaborate wit-play which is exposed in some early lines:

> I am no Poet here; my penne's the spout
> Where the rain-water of my eyes runs out.[31]

The next most important point we should notice about the pre-Peacham elegies is that almost all are written about, or dedicated to, people of high birth or position. The tendency reaches well back, to Greene,[32] for instance, with "Upon the Death of the right Honorable Sir Christopher Hatton Knight, late Lord Chancelor of England" in 1591. The poets were obviously sensitive on the subject. Webster[33] protested, "Nor gain nor praise by my weak lines are sought," in his lines to Prince Henry, and then proceeded to dedicate the poem to the infamous Sir Robert Carr. The elegies are a clear bid for favor and patronage. Peacham makes the same point in *An Aprill Shower,*[34] written on the Earl of Dorset and dedicated to his Countess:

> I heere professe, it is no by-regard,
> Or expectation of a slight reward
> Enforces me to weepe.

There is, however, significance in the fact that so many of the Prince Henry elegies prominently involve King James and Queen Anne. Other elegists do not look that high; but their eyes are seldom lowered beneath the level of nobility. Tourneur[35] writes on Sir Francis Vere; Drummond[36] on Sir Anthony Alexander [Alcon]; Milton on the Marchioness of Winchester; Christopher Brooke[37] on Sir Arthur Chichester (d. 1625); Waller[38] on Lady Rich; Jonson[39] on "Lady Jane Pawlet" and Lady Venetia Digby; Drayton[40] on Lady Clifton; Quarles on the Countess of Cleveland and "Lady Luckyn; and Carew[41] on Lady Anne Hay and "To the Countesse of Anglesie" on the death of her husband. Wither[42] chose to dedicate his "Henry" elegy to Robert Lord Sidney of Penshurst. John Taylor[43] was not to give Milton exclusive rights in honoring the "Sacred Memory of the . . . Lord Bishop of Winchester." Thus the innumerable elegies on Prince Henry are only typical. More significance is to be read in the fact that Donne appears to have hardly known the fifteen-year-old

Elizabeth Drury, but he clearly knew her wealthy and distinguished father, Sir Robert Drury. In the same way Peacham[44] himself confesses in "To the Reader" that he did not know well the Countess of Warwick about whom *Thestylis Atrata* was written, and had to get much of his impression of her secondhand. But at the same time he takes good care to dedicate the piece to Sir John Wray and Sir Christopher Wray.[45]

It is inevitable that we should derive our impression of early seventeenth-century elegies from the many that were written on Prince Henry. But before we examine those, we should look briefly at some that had others as their subjects. Naturally, there were memorials to King James and Queen Anne, though fewer than we might expect. Richard James'[46] "Muses Dirge" on the king, a thoroughly uninspired tribute with hackneyed classical paraphernalia such as Leda, Phoebus, Pandora, has inevitable religious leanings since its author was a minister. Its one interesting trait, in light of the elegiac tradition, is the amount of historical data interfused with the poetry. Little more can be said for John Taylor's[47] "Living Sadness" or Herbert of Cherbury's[48] unnotable "Epitaph." Chettle[49] and Phineas Fletcher[50] write mainly on the accession,[51] in connection with Queen Elizabeth's death. For the rest, James is brought in mainly to be consoled for the loss of Prince Henry. This is true of Thomas Campion's reference[52] and Chapman's,[53] though the latter is exceptional for the high praise he goes out of his way to give the king. Similarly, Peacham, in his *Prince Henrie Revived*[54] on the birth of Henry Frederick, expressly praises the child's grandfather.

Much the same may be said for James' Queen. To be sure, she had Latin elegies assembled for her at both the great universities,[55] and Patrick Hannay[56] has his two "Elegies on the Death of Our Late Soveraigne Queene Anne. With Epitaphs." Otherwise, she too enters to be consoled for Henry's death by Campion,[57] Wither,[58] and that evanescent figure Sir Arthur Gorges, who writes a sonnet in her honor to precede his elaborate *Olympian Catastrophe*.[59]

The elegies on Donne and Jonson belong somehow in a category of their own. This may be due in part to their having been conceived as literary criticism. Grierson[60] prints the ones on Donne and identifies many of the authors, making the point that most of them were young men.[61] Herbert of Cherbury sets the tone by emphasizing Donne's famed style, deploring the pretentious words of other tributes, and claiming that he will use the honest phraseology of the master's own language:[62]

> Nor will it serve, that thou did'st so refine
> Matter with words, that both did seem divine.

Izaak Walton[63] lays similar emphasis when he reminds England,

> Thou 'hast lost a man where language chose to stay
> And shew it's gracefull power.

And at the conclusion of his poem he draws an interesting distinction between Elizabethan and seventeenth-century elegies when he insists that he writes "no *Encomium,* but an *Elegie.*" Richard Brathwaite[64] is another who stresses Donne's intellectual side; to him he is "Prince of wits," and large claims are laid for his accomplishments:

> Of learning, languages, of eloquence,
> And Poësie, (past ravishing of sense,)
> He had a magazine.
>
> (ll. 21–23).

Brathwaite goes on to acknowledge his deep indebtedness to Donne in the matter of verse "whereof he was the master." Henry King[65] follows suit in a poem that, for its quality, should be better known.[66] The imagery is more memorable and gives the distinct impression of having been inspired by Donne himself. Henry King characterizes his subject as "Rich Soule of Witt and Language," and concludes:

> Who ever writes of Thee, and in a Stile
> Unworthy such a Theame, does but revile
> Thy precious Dust.
>
> (ll. 23–25).

Carew, like King, wrote notable tributes to both Donne and Jonson. His elegy on Donne is one of the finest pieces of verse criticism written in any language at any time; it is doubtful that any piece of Donne criticism has surpassed it. Here, Herbert of Cherbury's aspiration to write in Donne's own vigorous, honest language is clearly exemplified. Line after line could be lifted out of context without the reader's sensing any distinction from the Dean's own style. The words are the words of every day, but they are used with such telling effect as to make them seem fresh and new. Had Donne lived to read the elegy he might well have said in all his honesty,

"What a genius I had when I wrote those words!" It is not merely the holy rapes committed, the pedantic weeds, the masculine expression, the imperious wit, the rifled fields, thy just reign, new apostasy, reverend silence, dumb eloquence, impulsive force, devouring flashes, and universal monarchy of wit—not merely these, but the figures of which they form a part that make Carew's accomplishment so remarkable. The test comes when the reader says to himself, this is no elegy but a eulogy—the subject is still alive.

It is not fair to read Carew's "To Ben Jonson" after the Donne, or if we do so, we should conclude in Carew's own words about Ben:

> The wiser world doth greater thee confess
> Than all men else, than thyself only less.

Henry King's poem, on the other hand, is a real elegy. He calls it "To my Dead Friend Ben: Johnson,"[67] and it does not compare with his Donne in the personal element shown; in light of their close relationship, that was inevitable. It is almost as if King's awareness of Jonson's classicism kept feeling out. Ben is the symbol of one who has refined the language; he is

> Amongst those Soaring Wits that did dilate
> Our English, and advance it to the rate
> And value it now holdes: Thy self was one
> Helpt lift it up to such proportion,
> That thus Refin'd and Rob'd, It shall not spare
> With the full Greek or Latine to compare.

Obviously King has Jonson's own lines on Shakespeare in mind, as he does below when he writes, "Thy Book shall be Thy Tombe."[68]

Justa Edovardo King Naufrago came too late to have had any impact on Peacham's elegiac writing or indeed to have formed any part of the background against which he wrote. But it still must be considered briefly. The usual evaluation of it is that Milton's "Lycidas" stands out like a multi-carat diamond in the midst of marcasite. Actually the other contributions are not all that bad, particularly when compared with many elegies produced in the first part of the seventeenth-century. As it happened, most of the contributors to this volume on Edward King were in their early twenties—some years younger than Milton.

Miss Wallerstein[69] has a very good analysis of some of the pieces, concentrating particularly on Joseph Beaumont, Cleveland,

and William More. She finds Beaumont's effort a rather formal and conventional poem dominated by rationalism, with a resultant lack of personal feeling. It combines the familiar *de contemptu* theme with a portrait of Edward King as a type of virtue, and at the end the usual *consolatio*. She quite properly classifies Beaumont among the allegorists and emblematists. Cleveland, on the other hand, side-steps the consolation and resists presenting King as representative of virtue. Here again, the wit-play is so prominent that it overshadows the description of King's personal character. Of course, his brother Henry's tribute stands apart in all this. W. More deplores the very wit-play in which Cleveland indulges, though, paradoxically, he has his own type of word-play. The most arresting portion of his elegy is the passage where he compares King's calmness in the face of death with Christ's similar experience. On the poems as a whole Miss Wallerstein[70] draws the following conclusion: "They assert Providence, the beauty of King's character, the social ideal, the punishment of our sins by the loss of King." She especially notes in most the absence of the pastoral element. And thus Milton is, as usual, the great exception, still under the spell of his acknowledged "original," Spenser.

If we can safely pass by *Justa Edovardo King Naufrago* with little more than a nod, we must on the contrary examine with great care the numerous elegies written on Prince Henry.[71] Coming as they did in 1612 and 1613, they could not help setting the tone of elegies for at least the whole first half of the seventeenth century. Milton himself could not have missed their importance.[72] E. C. Wilson in his interesting book *Prince Henry and English Literature*[73] rightly calls these elegies "the fullest elegiac chorus of his [Milton's] lifetime." And this applies just as well to Peacham. It has to be remembered first that, though these poems were written on a Prince, most other elegies concerned people of noble blood and were written in part to curry favor and patronage. Therefore the Henry poems should not be regarded as the great exception.

A kind of Kennedy myth had grown up around Prince Henry even before he died.[74] It should not be questioned that the prince was a remarkable young man.[75] But he was invested with every virtue in the book. The tone is set by a passage in *Chesters triumph in honor of her prince*[76] (1610) where Mercury is sent down to confer on Henry the blessings of all the gods:

And know (deere Sir) thy deedes and good deserts,
Thy well disposed Nature, Minde, and thought,
Thy zealous care to keepe their Lawes divine,
Thy great compassion on poore wights distrest,
Thy prudence, justice, temp'rance, and thy truth,
And, to be briefe, thy vertues generall,
Have mov'd them all from Heav'n, with one assent,
To send Me downe, to let thee understand
That thou art highly in their Favors plac'd.

It is significant, however, that the elegists tended to concentrate on comparatively few of these prime qualities. There were certain ways in which Henry was regularly thought of by his contemporaries. All knew him to be the great Elizabeth's godson, and they knew as well that he took over his godmother's active support of literature. George Chapman was rewarded with being "sewer in ordinary" to Henry.[77] The prince promised him the tidy sum of £300 and, on his death bed, added a life pension. All along, Henry encouraged the poet in his work on Homer, and it was therefore only natural that Chapman should dedicate his second installment (1609) to the "Great Prince of men." It is to be hoped that Henry was as favorably impressed as Keats when he first looked into Chapman's Homer. In much the same way Ralegh sought encouragement. A close relationship had grown up between them,[78] which Ralegh acknowledged in dedications; and Henry obviously followed with care the progress on *The History of the World*. The historian is quite explicit on this point: "For it was for the service of that inestimable prince Henry, the successive hope, and one of the greatest of the Christian world, that I undertook this work. It pleased him to peruse some part thereof, and to pardon what was amiss. It is now left to the world without a master." At the end he explains that the second and third volumes which he had planned were not forthcoming because of their sponsor's death. It is well known that Henry moved heaven and earth to induce James to release Ralegh from the Tower.

Jonson was brought close to the prince in a different way; his *Oberon, or the Fairy Prince* was intended to honor Henry.[79] Oberon was obviously identified with him, and Henry returned the honor by acting the lead role in the 1611 performance at Whitehall. Furthermore, the prince got so interested in *The Masque of Queens* (1609) that he asked Jonson to explain the learned allusions. When the masque appeared in print the poet dedicated it to his patron with a lengthy and ringing tribute, especially praising his "favor to letters, and these gentler studies, that goe under the title of Humanitye." He concludes by promising to "labor to bring forth some worke as worthy of your fame, as my ambition therein is of your pardon." There is an un-Jonsonian warmth about the whole piece that transcends all convention. Bacon[80] added his dedication in a letter to precede the 1612 edition of his *Essays*. He wrote[81] that Henry "was fond of antiquity and arts: and a favourer of learning, though rather in the honour he paid it than the time he spent upon it." Drayton dedicated the first part of his *Polyolbion* to Henry. E. C. Wilson[82] has discovered over one hundred and twenty-five books dedicated to the prince.

When Professor Wilson[83] says that "no elegy occasioned by Henry's death achieves greatness,"[84] we cannot but agree. Obviously there is no *Lycidas* among them. At the same time, such a remark may be misleading, for there are individual passages that rank high. And while we have a tendency to be condescending, we should recall the circumstances under which the elegies were produced. These men were all in the rôle of poets laureate *pro tem,* all subject to command performance. Not merely did they have to pay tribute to a fantastically popular prince, but, what made matters worse, they had to keep in mind the impression they were making on their subject's royal father and mother. That was a task to awe the greatest of poets; it may be one reason why Shakespeare never made his contribution.

For the collection as a whole, Miss Wallerstein[85] has summarized the qualities, from the philosophic point of view: "Spenser with his Renaissance and humanist Christian Platonism, Donne with his theology, his dialectic, and his troubled devotion, dominate all that is most significant in the Prince Henry elegies." As for the form, there is an extraordinary variety in the verse used;[86] it is as if some of the poets chose the occasion to experiment metrically.

The large number of poets who chose to write elegies on the occasion of Henry's death is impressive. The following is a partial list (besides Peacham): John Davies of Hereford, Wither, John Taylor, Rowley, Tourneur, Heywood, Webster, Giles Fletcher, Phineas Fletcher, Jonson, Donne, Herbert of Cherbury, Drummond, Henry King, Joshua Sylvester, James Maxwell, Richard Brathwaite, William Fennor, William Browne, Sir Henry Goodyere, George Gerrard, Christopher Brooke, John Ward, Sir John Hayward, Sir William Alexander, Robert Allyne, William Basse, Thomas Campion, Richard Niccols, Sir Arthur Gorges, and Patrick Gordon. In addition, there were dozens of Henry elegies in Greek and Latin, as well as English, issued at Oxford and Cambridge.

The next thing that impresses us is that the eulogists appear to have had a tacit agreement to emphasize three of Henry's characteristics: as a warrior and active participant in tournaments; as a religionist who would wage the Protestant battle against Romanism; as a scholar and patron of learning.[87] Naturally, each poet had his particular way of presenting these traits.

It fed the Jacobean sense of nationalism to think of Henry in terms of their great heroes; they all but conferred upon him the title of Prince Hal II. This meant that they would naturally inherit from the earlier age the tendency to consider their reigning sovereigns as direct successors to King Arthur himself. In the Jonson masque already mentioned, Oberon [Henry] is saluted as heir of Arthur's "crown and chair."[88] At about the same time Peacham presented to Henry a Latin translation of his own emblems, greeting the Prince as Arthur *redux*.[89] Lines beneath an emblem picture of a warrior in full armor express the hope that Henry will emulate Alexander the Great. But Henry's eulogists did not stop there; to find parallels they had to go far back in history. Drummond[90] eulogizes:

> A youth more brave pale Troy with trembling walls
> Did never see.

The inevitable comparison, however, was with the god Mars himself. John Taylor[91] refers to Henry, "Whose valor brav'd the mighty God of Armes." The acme—or the nadir—is reached when Wither,[92] in his "Elegiak-sonnets," writes, "*Mars* himselfe envi'd his future glory." If Henry had fought shoulder-to-shoulder with the Black Prince at Crécy, he could hardly have won more praise.[93] Davies of Hereford[94] goes so far as to say,

> In all exercise of *Armes* he was
> Unmatch'd by any of his yeares.

There can be no question that Henry reveled in trappings of the tournament. On the other hand, there can be no question that Englishmen, as they watched his jousting, had their vision so transmogrified that they were actually seeing him as a medieval knight in full armor charging with spear couched. This picture comes through clear in Campion's description:[95]

> His Launce appear'd to the beholders eyes,
> When his faire hand advaunc't it to the skyes,
> Larger then truth, for well could hee it wield,
> And make it promise honour in the field
> (11. 23–26).

Henry's physical activities must have been extraordinary:

> To Vault and leap, to wrestle, ride and runne
> . . . .
> To runne at Ring, at Tilt and Turnament.[96]

And Brooke[97] gives us another memorable picture of Henry leaving orders to be waked at dawn, and mounting "his hot steede, shining in glorious armes." Sir Arthur Gorges[98] is the one, however, who presents the most complete description. Almost in the manner of the *Knight's Tale,* he gives details of costumes and much of the paraphernalia associated with medieval tournaments. Henry contends with another noble, performs magnificently, and, of course, carries off the prize. And when the prince dies, Wither[99] asks,

> Who now shall grace my turnaments:
> Or honour me [Mars] with deeds of Chivalry?

In the good tradition of the Italian courtier, Henry was interested in horses and horsemanship.[100] In fact, as James Maxwell[101] says, his ambition was "to ride great horses, and to handle armes."

The interest regularly paired with war and tournaments was learning. This meant that Mars and Minerva were as inseparable as Castor and Pollux:

> By day *Mars* held his launce, by night
> *Minerva* bore a torch to give him light.[102]

The legend went that Henry took care to divide his time equally. Thus, Brooke[103] is quite explicit:

> His time by equall portions he divided
> Betweene his bookes and th' exercise of warre.

Thomas Heywood[104] sounds the same note when he insists that the Prince's "aime was to know *Art* and Chivalry." Obviously he repeats the idea in other words with "He was halfe *Love,* halfe *Warre.*" Gorges sums it all up in *The Olympian Catastrophe*[105] when he calls Minerva and Bellona to bestow their respective gifts on royal Henry. It would be natural for Thomas Campion[106] to make art equivalent to music: "When Court and Musicke cal'd him, off fell armes." It may be seriously questioned, from what we know from other sources about Henry's character, whether he was quite so meticulous in seeing that books got half his time.

As it happens, Peacham[107] succeeds in summing up all the qualities normally associated with Henry:

> The worlds sole wonder and delight,
> The richest Jemme ere *Nature* wrought
> For prizeles forme, of purest thought,
> For chast desire, for Churches zeale,
> For care and love of common weale;
> For manly shape, for active might,
> For Courage and Heroique sprit,
> For Love of Armes and Heavenly Arts.

James Maxwell[108] takes care in his first epigram to record the two qualities most often attributed to the prince, "the Soldiers solace, and the Schollars joy."[109] Of these two characteristics, poets were naturally apt to emphasize, *over*emphasize, the latter. As we have seen,[109a] Henry had built for himself an enviable reputation as a patron of learning. Peacham fully acknowledges his own debt to Henry in his dedication of *Minerva Britanna*[110] to the Prince: "Having by more then ordinarie signes, tasted heeretofore of your gratious favour: and evidently knowen your *Princely* and *Generous* inclination, to all good Learning and excellencie . . ." He goes on to remind Henry that two years previously he had presented him with some emblems in a volume of Latin translations from James' own *Basilicon Doron* in which he, Peacham, had included "pictures drawen and limned by mine owne hand in their lively coulours." His gratitude is further expressed in the following lines:[111]

> Thus under that sweete shadow of your winges,
> Best loves the Artes, and Innocence to build:
> And thus my Muse, that never saf'tie knew,
> With weary wing, great HENRIE flies to you.

The British Museum[112] has a picture, "much oxidised," of Henry, holding his sword erect, sitting on a plumed horse, and in the lower right-hand corner there is an inscription "Henr. Peacham f." Miss Pitman[113] lists the item in her section under Manuscripts and says it was prefixed to a treatise called "Le Pourtraict de Monseigneur le Prince."

Like Peacham, James Maxwell[114] does not hesitate to call Henry "great *Mecenas* of the *Muses* nine," just as Webster[115] refers to him as "grave *Mecaenas* of the noble Arts." Wither[116] is similarly grief-stricken when he laments, "my hope-fulst Patron's dead" and follows by declaring "I lov'd him as my *Prince:* as *Henry* more." In general, it may be said that Wither puts more personal feeling than most into *Prince Henries Obsequies.* It is conceivable that others felt that there would be an element of *lèse-majesté* in such familiarity. But poets sensed what an irreparable loss to their calling Henry's early death was. Some even declared that doomsday had come. Chapman[117] wrote:

> Mourne all ye Arts, ye are not of the earth;
> Fall, fall with him;

and Gorges[118] said much the same:

> For arts grew fainte when this sweet Prince was dead,
> That in his life tyme them with bountie fedd.

Peacham, in *The Period of Mourning,*[119] has also represented Henry in his First Vision as a "goodly Arke,"

> In whom the Hopes of many thousands were,
> But chiefly of the Muse.

In the *Epicedium*[120] which follows, he refers to "Henrie Loadstar of the Arts," and in the still later "Elegiack Epitaph upon . . . Prince Henrie"[121] he reemphasized it by attributing to him a "Love of Armes and Heavenly Arts."[122] Davies of Hereford[123] made a special point of saying:

> With *Arts* and *Letters* hee so stor'd his *Mind*
> That both knew all therein, y'er *Youth* could know.

Heywood[124] is perhaps the most courageous of all the elegists when he writes what could not but be interpreted as a gratuitous piece of advice to Prince Charles:

> Princes swords
> Should defend *Art,* and *Art* make Princes wise.

Peacham was fully conscious of the third quality so often mentioned; among the *vales* which conclude his *Epicedium* he has:[125] "Farewell the Church and Learnings prop." Heywood[126] writes in this same vein when he says that Henry ardently pursued art and chivalry, "Save when to heaven he did his vowes betake."[127] The Prince was clearly looked upon as the great champion of Protestantism.[128] In fact, Robert Allyne[129] roundly berates Death for having prevented Henry from overwhelming "Antichristian Rome" and from having,

> throwne downe the walles of Rome,
> And layde them levell with the lowest ground.

How deep the feeling ran is to be inferred from the ferocity of the language. Richard Niccols[130] confidently believed that the prince would have driven Rome to the wall and hunted "hence *Romes* Rats." Wither[131] is no more complimentary with his "Romes Locusts." It is these two poets also who emphasize Henry's firmness of purpose, the former[132] insisting that he was "Religions stedfast friend, and Errors foe," the latter[133] protesting that among his many noble qualities he noticed none more "than in *Religion* his firme constant minde." Further, in *Prince Henries Obsequies*[134] Wither visualizes Henry's arms "advanc't above the Capitoll of *Rome*." To all appearances Rome and Spain stood in terror of him,[135] Wither[136] making him out a kind of Sir Francis Drake because "*Spaine* trembled" at his very name. With this profound interest in fostering the right religion, Campion[137] combines a parallel interest in colonization:

> his care had beene
> Survaying India, and implanting there
> The knowledge of that God which hee did feare
> (11. 50–52).

But it is Drummond[138] who expresses most forcefully England's bitter regret:

> If Heaven (alas) ordain'd thee young to die,
> Why was it not where thou thy Might did'st trie?
> . . . .
> Moeliades, ô that by Isters Streames,
> Amongst shrill-sounding Trumpets, flaming gleames
> Of warme encrimson'd Swords, and Cannons Roare,

Balls thicke as Raine pour'd by the Caspian Shore,
Amongst crush'd Lances, ringing Helmes, and Shields,
Dismembred Bodies ravishing the Fields,
In Turkish Blood made red like Marses Starre,
Thou ended hadst thy Life, and Christian Warre!
Or, as brave Bourbon, thou hadst made old Rome,
Queen of the world, thy triumph's place and tomb!

There are a few other themes that course through the elegies. One is the declared inability of the poet to express the depth of his grief. Wither[139] finds his Muse totally unequal to the great task, as does Ralegh: "Impossible it is to equal words and sorrows."[140] Henry King[141] expresses the same thought by resort to an unusual word, "unable Poetry." Gorges'[142] extreme language paradoxically becomes almost humorous in its extravagance:

My Muse did want her selle, my sence was numbe,
My heart grew fainte, my quicker power grew slow,
Myne eyes were dimme, my tongue was taken dumbe,
My inke no longer from my penn would flowe,
For inke, tongue, eyes, power, hart, senc, muse, apawld,
Became thick, dumbe, dymme, slow, faint, nume, and stald.[143]

If their grief was inexpressible, however, the elegists appear to have had no trouble in expressing their hatred of Death for having taken away their idol. Here their language becomes at times violent; to render their attack effective they had to make Death *live*. To Taylor[144] he is "man-murdring, blinde, cruell, fierce and fell," a "robustuous rawbon'd monster"; to Webster[145] he is "cruel tyrant." Wither[146] refers to his "tyranny," to his being "cruell and insatiable," and Thomas Heywood[147] to his "fell tyranny." In his *Funerall Elegie*[148] Heywood goes on to curse "the fatall Dames."[149] The one way in which Death was ever justified was that it naturally thought Henry, with his mature qualities, to be older than he was. This is the approach taken by Basse:[150]

Time, looking on his wisdom, thought him old,
And laid his rash Sythe to his Primest yeares.

Drayton[151] says almost the same about Lady Stanhope, Nature regarding "thy wisedome, not thy youth," and so took her away "thinking thou wast old." Brooke[152] rephrases the same idea:

God measures not His gifts by age or yeares,
His sence was hoarie although greene his haires.

If it was not the wisdom of the deceased which was eulogized, it was his other virtues. This is what Donne[153] stresses when writing of Lady Marckham "lest they that heare her vertues, thinke her old." And Crashaw[154] does the same with his "Mr. Herrys":

numbring of his vertues praise,
Death lost the reckoning of his Dayes;
And believing what they told,
Imagin'd him exceeding old.

Thus, Jonson's well-turned tribute to the child actor, Solomon Pavy, must be regarded as in a tradition:

And did act, what now we moan,
Old men so duly,
As, sooth, the Parcae thought him one,
He played so truly.

Another theme that emerges from time to time is that England, for her sins, deserves the loss of Henry. Basse[155] charges his country to stop weeping for the prince and to begin weeping for her own sins, "which made Heav'n *Henry* take." Sylvester[156] makes the point even more forcefully when he advises people to shed no tears for him who is better off, but rather to weep for themselves in their sins. Sylvester[157] makes another interesting point when he says that God often takes away good princes for people's sins, the opposite of the well-recognized belief that bad princes are sent upon countries for their sins. Wither[158] protests that England had fair warning but persisted in her sins, and Heywood[159] is equally explicit. In his poem[160] addressed to Henry's sister, the Princess Elizabeth, he devotes about the first fifty lines to the prince himself:

Is it because we breake the gods decree
That, Tantalus, we are punisht like to thee
. . . .
So have the gods dealt with us for some crime.

The elegists are just as apt to give the other side of the picture; Death and England may have been to blame, but Heaven wanted Henry and he is better off there anyway. Both Sylvester and Alexander have as an important part of their themes that Heaven was calling for its own. Sylvester[161] maintained that the prince was too good for this world; Alexander[162] that it was fortunate he died while standing so high in the estimation of everyone. Drummond and Brooke use two significant terms to convey Heaven's attitude, the former[163] uses "envious," the latter,[164] "jealous" ("For Heav'n is *jealous* of the world's delight"). Gorges[165] visualizes Jove (God) taking the Prince "to his high bower," and Chapman[166] comes as close to scolding God as he dares:

O God, to what end are thy Graces given?
Onely to show the world, Men fit for Heaven,
Then ravish them, as if too good for Earth?

The corollary to all this is that the person is better off in Heaven. Sylvester[167] is quite explicit on the point, and Heywood[168] is equally dogmatic. Basse[169] writes, "now He in Heav'n doth rest," and Giles Fletcher[170] notices that "our Prince is now in heav'n a King," visualizing God and Christ as a welcoming party at the Golden Gates. This is, in fact, the grand finale of his poem. Maxwell[171] uses his own powers of visualization to observe Henry as he plucks flowers in Paradise; and the upshot of the whole first part of his "Memorable Life and Death" is that the Prince belongs more in Heaven than on earth. It is no wonder, therefore, that in *A Poetical Rhapsody,* Oberon [Henry] is represented as "a glorious Saint in heaven."[172] Webster[173] introduces another element when he says that Henry is glad to die to escape the nothingness of the world. This *de contemptu mundi* theme is pursued at considerable length by Arthur Gorges in his *Olympian Catastrophe:*[174]

Tis but polluting-pitch that doth defile
The soule: tis but a snare that doth enthrall:
Tis nought but clammy lyme, that doth beguile
The silly birds: a nett that tangles all,
For all are tangeled, caught, enthralled, beguild;
And by this nett, snare, lyme, and pitch defild.

His summation comes in the lines:

The crowne he had, was but a type of care:
The crowne he hath is joyes eternall seale.

Drummond[175] is somewhat more specific about the ills Henry has escaped and about the more ideal conditions he finds in Heaven:

Courts void of flattery, of malice minds,
Pleasure which lasts, not such as reason blinds:
Far sweeter songs thou hear'st and carollings.

Peacham,[176] in his *Elegiacke Epitaph upon . . . Prince Henrie,* is remarkably close here while expressing his own contempt for hangers-on at court:

When Parasite, nor Spangled groome,
With Courtiers vaine accloy thy roome.

One final element should be noticed: the tendency of many an elegist to speak in terms of extravagance and hyperbole. William Browne's title alone is symptomatic: *An Elegie on the Never Inough Bewailed Death of the Worthy, Vertuous, glory of these, and wonder for ensuing times, Henry, Prince of Wales.*[177] Something of the attitude may be gathered from Gorges'[178] having written, "For Henries very name, my sence distracts." Henry King[179] thought that the world would suffer less on doomsday than on the day of Henry's death, and Wither[180] is equally of the opinion that loss of the prince is far worse than the ravages of the late plague. To Heywood[181] it is the greatest tragedy ever. Both Giles Fletcher[182] and William Browne[183] believe that England has now lost her claim to the title of a Fortunate Isle. Such adulation results in Sylvester's lines:[184]

O Dearest! Cleerest! Purest! Surest *Prop!*
O Gravest! Bravest! Highest! Nighest Hope.

The extent of this praise may be seen in the passage where Gorges[185] has Mercury come down from Heaven to express the gods' approval:

To our Idea, natures quintessence,
The Gods Epitome, Fames Pyramis,
The all of Art, and Armes, the all of sence,
The all of Glorye, and of worldlie blisse,
For blisse, and glory, arms, arts, Fame and all,
Fell, when this Pyramid did take his fall.[186]

Alexander[187] says that he may have been "by nature" the king's son, but "by adoption Gods." As if this were not enough, Giles Fletcher[188] elevates the prince to a relative of God:

Bedded in all the roses of delight
Let thy engladded soule embalmed lie,
Imbrightned into that celestiall light,

Which all Gods saintly Lamps doth glorifie,
Thear boast thy kinred with the Deitie
Whear God his Sonne, and Christ his Brother greet thee.

Fairly typical are the lines in Davies'[189] *Muses Teares:*

He was the richest *Trophey Fortunes* Pow'r
Could reare in *Honors* Theater; for, stil
Nature did doate on *Him* (her *Bellamoure,*
Or *Master-peece,* the Wonder of her skil![190]

Miss Wallerstein,[191] in her remarks on Donne's elegy, refers to "the gross exaggeration of its adulation." Considering what some other elegists wrote, all that can be said is that more might have been expected from John Donne.

To all of this there was naturally a reaction. The elegy by "G. G."[192] (probably Donne's friend, George Gerrard) deplores the excesses. And W. More and Herbert of Cherbury follow suit, the former in his poem on Edward King,[193] the latter[194] in his elegy on Donne, where he protests that he is sick of overblown, pretentious words and declares that he will use more honest phraseology in imitation of the great stylist whose tribute he is writing.

It was inevitable that Henry's name should be linked with his sister's; they appear to have stood unusually close. When Elizabeth married the Elector Palatine and went with him to live in Heidelberg, James Maxwell[195] wrote:

In one yeare, we drinke of double woes;
By loosing first our Lilly, then our Rose.

It was not unusual for poets to combine the death and the marriage as Peacham did in his *Period of Mourning* when he added in that same volume his *Nuptiall Hymnes: In Honour of the Marriage.* Thus immediately following his *Great Brittaines Sunnes-set,* Basse[196] has a poem with the significant title *A Morning After Mourning,* honoring the Princess' marriage. Allyne[197] has the same combination in his *Teares of Joy* where he pays high tribute to Prince Henry before launching into his praise of the nuptial pair at their departure from Britain. Wither[198] refers to Elizabeth in his *Obsequies;* Heywood praises her in his *Funerall Elegie;*[199] and Gorges writes her a sonnet to precede his *Olympian Catastrophe.* Just as naturally, poems on the princess contain references to her brother. Heywood's[200] is a fairly typical combination:

> Now the wet winter of our teares is past,
> And see, the cheerefull Spring appeares at last;
> Now may we calculate by the welkins racke,
> Aeolus hath chaste the clouds that were so blacke,
> And th' are beyond the hyperboreans runne
> That have so late eclipst Great Brittaines sonne.

The other note sometimes sounded is one of consolation for the grieving sister.[201] But the most original approach of all is taken by William Fennor[202] who, after declaring,

> This hopefull match begot great gladnesse,
> But *Henries* death a solemne sadnesse,

practically says that if England had enjoyed both Henry's continued existence and the happy marriage of his sister, it might have died from the excess! In his dedication to *The Period of Mourning,*[203] Peacham speaks of how much he owed to the prince, but at the same time he acknowledges his great debt to "the Princesse my most gracious Lady." And two years later when he dedicates *Prince Henrie Revived*[204] to Elizabeth, he begins, "Sithence it hath pleased your Highnesse, heeretofore to take notice of me and my labours. . . ."

The reason the Elector's name is sometimes associated with that of the prince is that Frederick was thought of as taking Henry's place. For instance, Robert Allyne in his *Teares of Joy*[205] writes, "A *Fredericke* in his losse, supplies his roome"; and then, addressing the Elector, says that Henry, "left not the world, till thou assum'd his place." And similarly in *A Morning After Mourning,*[206] William Basse declares that "a second Sonne in Henries place doth shine." Contemporaries noted that at the time of his death Henry was making every preparation to receive his future brother-in-law and "to grace [him] with all possible honour."

The issue of that noteworthy marriage was expected to fulfill Henry's promise. William Fennor wrote in that great hope:

> And eare twelve monethes their course had run
> Betwixt them they possest a Sonne.
>
> . . . .
>
> From *Henry's* ashes, there is sprung,
> A second *Henry*.[207]

It was in this mood that Peacham wrote his own *Prince Henrie Revived,* protesting that only this hopeful birth inspired him to take up again his pen which had been laid away "in silence."[208] So great were Peacham's expectations that he visualized the new Henry becoming another Arthur.[209] In the fourth nuptial hymn[210] he has Venus say:

> And let me live to see betweene you twaine,
> A *Caesar* borne as great as *Charlemaine.*

Henry's younger brother, Charles, (later Charles I) was unfortunate from the beginning, cast into shadow by his elder brother's splendor. Some accounts did say that at least he enjoyed his brother's affection; there "was never one that loved his brother more deerely then our peerelesse Prince *Henry* did his brother Duke *Charles.*"[211] But one gets the impression that such compliments were turned in the elder's direction. In other words, Charles played a pale Troilus to Henry's Hector. It is true that poets such as Maxwell[212] and Wither[213] praise Charles. But again it is with the thought that he may reflect some of Henry's glory. Peacham was to write years later in *An Aprill Shower*[214] (1624):

> What Cunning Artistes pencill may I borrow,
> Thrice-hopefull *Charles* to limne thy griefe and sorrow.

PEACHAM AND THE ELEGY

Peacham's own contribution to the Henry elegies was, of course, *The Period of Mourning. Disposed into sixe Visions. In Memorie of the late Prince* (1613). There appears to be some question as to just when he composed his memorial lines to Henry, though he clearly wrote after many of the elegists. It is too simple an explanation to say he waited until after Princess Elizabeth's marriage in order to combine his *Nuptiall Hymnes* with the elegy. He does say[1] in addressing his Muse, "Thou hast been asleepe." Wherever the truth may lie, he subjoined to *The Period* an "Epicedium"[2] which is defined in the note as being "proper to the body while it is unburied," and a six-line addendum which he entitled "To the buried Prince."[3] Those are followed by "An Elegiacke *Epitaph* upon the untimely death of the hopefull Prince *Henrie,* etc. Written by the Author, at the time of his Death."[4] We shall never know whether all this paraphernalia was designed to excuse his dilatoriness. Peacham was well aware of how much he owed to Henry, and he so expresses himself in his dedication to *The Period* where he mentions "my love to his excellent vertues, and person, to whom I was so many wayes engaged." In his *vale* in "Epicedium"[5] he writes, "Farewell the arme that held me up."

To be fully understood, *The Period* must be placed beside the many other elegies written on the occasion. In comparing it with another elegy, Miss Wallerstein[6] speaks of "the altogether more accomplished laments of Henry Peacham. . . . In Peacham's poems, on the other hand, the emotion rising from the style is in itself the substance of the lament." She continues, describing his verses as "closely imitating the texture of Spenser's style." Later in her study,[7] she implies that Peacham's influence may have caused Henry More at mid-century to favor the Spenserian style. In other poems Peacham showed that he was fully conscious of the magic of the Spenserian stanza. In *Prince Henrie Revived*[8] the complimentary verses to Princess Elizabeth which follow the Dedication are in the stanza, eight decasyllables and an Alexandrine, though the rhyme scheme is slightly different.

Obviously Peacham was aware of the "vision" literature of the Middle Ages.[9] But he was equally aware of Spenser's paraphrases from Petrarch and Du Bellay. He knew that there were six visions in "Petrarch" and he has six visions in *The Period*.[10] In Vision III[11] he has a picture that bears resemblance to Spenser's famous Cave of Despair:[12]

> A Wood there was, along the *Stygian* Lake,
> Where *Night,* and everlasting *Horror* dwell,
> Herein a Cave, two hollow Rockes did make,
> From whence a Brooke as blacke as *Lethe* fell:
> . . . .
> It was an uncouth Dungeon, darke and wide,
> Where living man nere was, or light had shone,
> Save that a little glimmering I espi'de
> From rotten stickes, that all about were throwne:
> The Boxe and banefull Eugh-tree grew without,
> All which a stinking ditch did moate about.

The "light had shone, Save that a little glimmering I espi'de" can hardly help recalling Spenser's description of Red Cross Knight at Error's cave:[13]

> his glistring armor made
> A litle glooming light. . . .
> By which he saw . . .

Peacham's "two hollow Rockes" are like Spenser's "hollow cave" of Despair. Despair's "raw-bone cheekes, through penurie and pine" are like Death, who "was with pine become a Sceleton." In fact, Spenser's "cursed man" discovered "low sitting on the ground, Musing full sadly in his sullein mind" is like Peacham's.

> In mid'st there sat a meagre wretch alone,
> That had in sorrow both his ei'n outwept.[14]

In the next Vision (IV) Una appears, and the note defines her as "Unitie." There is a certain resemblance between Una's "Carre Triumphall, all of massie Gold" and Pride's coach[15] adorned all with gold," though, as Professor John Livingston Lowes was fond of saying, it is all *mutatis mutandis* since Una's conveyance is drawn by "foure fierce Lyons" and Lucifera's by "six unequall beasts." Miss Pitman[16] comments on Vision V: "The 'pastoral convention', whereby Peacham approaches his subject in the fifth 'vision', bears traces of having passed through Spenser's hands."

Throughout there are similarities of material and language which are, to say the least, disturbing and intriguing—more, perhaps, than one would expect from two poets working quite independent of each other. Some of the material is obviously contraband. Two Englishmen would naturally think of the metaphor of wrecked ships. And yet there is something in the way they are introduced and an occasional reminiscence of language that gives one pause. Peacham[17] begins his "visions" with a ship, "Whose Sayles were Silke, and Tackle twined Oare." Spenser-Petrarch[18] has "sailes of golde, of silke the tackle were." Both ships are wrecked on rocks. Spenser has other shipwrecks in "Bellay"[19] and in "Visions of the Worlds Vanitie,"[20] though, significantly, in the latter case it is "Remora" that wrecks the ship.

Much the same may be said about the analogy with trees as symbols of decay. In Vision II[21] Peacham has a palm tree and makes a special point of mentioning the singing birds, before "it downe with hideous fragor fell." Spenser (or his originals) seems almost possessed with trees as a symbol of decay. In "Petrarch"[22] there is a laurel tree:

> Such store of birds therein yshrowded were,
> Chaunting in shade their sundrie melodie,
> That with their sweetnes I was ravish't nere.

In "Visions of the Worlds Vanitie"[23] Spenser has a cedar destroyed by a "litle wicked worme." Peacham's tree succumbs to "a fearefull Serpent." In "Ruines of Rome"[24] Spenser-Bellay has a "great oke" that is similarly "meate of wormes."

We know that at times Peacham grew profoundly disillusioned with life; but again one wonders whether some of the indigo might have been poured from Spenser's "Visions." Peacham goes well beyond Prince Henry when in his sixth "vision"[25] he has the other princes sitting. "To view their worldly miseries foregone, Their

Kingdomes changes." In the previous stanza he has mentioned the great Roman monuments, all destined to decay, and one is again reminded of "Ruines of Rome." If this line runs through Peacham's "Visions," it is more prominent still in the "Epitaph"[26] which follows. Here he has:

> And bid'st Adiew these heapes of clay,
> Cares restles roomes, Innes for a day.
> Oh that the Heavens deny it me,
> Here loathing life, to follow thee!

Spenser is as outspoken. In "Petrarch"[27] he has "loath this base world." And in the previous stanza he wrote:

> Alas! on earth so nothing doth endure,
> But bitter griefe and sorrowfull annoy:
> Which make this life wretched and miserable.

He continues:

> When I behold this tickle trustles state
> Of vaine worlds glorie, flitting too and fro,
> And mortall men tossed by troublous fate
> In restles seas of wretchednes and woe,
> I wish I might this wearie life forgoe.[28]

He is no more cheerful in the conclusion he draws in "Bellay":[29] "Alas! this world doth nought but grievance hold."

In "Vision VI," the last, there are further resemblances to the Spenserian paraphrases. For instance, in stanza three,[30] Peacham has a "Theater of gold" and it is "on a mount." In "Bellay"[31] Spenser's impressive structure is on "high hills top" and it is embellished with gold: "hundred steps of Afrike golds enchase," "great plates of golde," "Golde was the parget."[32] Peacham has "stately columnes"; Spenser has "stately frame" and "hundreth pillours." Peacham has "Rockes of Diamond"; Spenser has "all wrought with diamond." Peacham has "Christall lights that shone"; Spenser has "shining christall" that threw "a thousand rayons." What we have done is to compare just two stanzas. In the following stanza Peacham wrote, "And *seel'd* [italics mine] with silke of starry gilt in blew." The eighteenth-century editor felt that he had to explain "seel'd": "*i.e.* ciel'd, as we now spell it; from Ciel, the French for Heav'n." In that same stanza Spenser has "Golde was the parget, and the seeling bright." If the editor had known Spenser's version, perhaps he would have regarded his note as supererogatory.

In view of the above evidence, it is not too much to claim for Henry Peacham that he deserves to stand, with the Fletchers and William Browne, as one more stepping-stone between Spenser and the seventeenth century.[33]

In his opening "Vision" Peacham adapts a convention to the particular occasion by picturing a shipwreck. Prince Henry's interest in ships and shipping must have begun early; when he was only ten, a master shipwright was commissioned to make for him a miniature ship.[34] Thomas Birch records this interest, "for which he afterwards shewed a strong inclination."[35] It was also said that he was "so well addicted to his Majesty's ships and the sight of them."[36] As a crowning tribute to his interest a great ship was built just for him: Peacham has the lines,[37]

> She *Archôn* hight, for that she had no Peere,
> And could command the *Ocean* with her might.[38]

Much is made in the contemporary accounts[39] of the prince's going to Woolwich to view the launching of his man-of-war, which he christened the "Prince Royal." It was the largest vessel ever built in England, and it was said that if all units of the fleet had been her equal, England would never have had to fear foreign rivals. Peacham wrote: "Brave Man of warre she was, from *Britaine* bound." She set out to sea "With sound of Trumpet" as Henry was received with "drums and trumpets." On an earlier, very important occasion, of which much is made in the narratives, the prince was honored with "salutes from thirty-one great brass chambers. The prince was doubly delighted because he had not expected the firing."[40] Peacham has:

> Such peales of Thunder, then anone were sent,
> As if she would have torne the Firmament.

He further speaks of the great ship *"Archôn's"* being bound, "For new discoveries all that might be found." Henry's interest in discovery and colonization was well known. He was deeply involved in finding the northwest passage to the East.[41] As formally constituted supreme protector of the enterprise, he personally chose the captain to lead the expedition. Being intimately associated with the Virginia Company,[42] he was instrumental in getting Thomas Dale sent to Jamestown. In 1607 a journal of Newport's voyage was sent back to

Henry.[43] For his enthusiastic interest he was known as the protector and patron of the colony for his "royall heart was ever strongly affected to that action."[44] In gratitude the colonists named a town "Henrico" after him as well as "Cape Henry." It was even planned that a university be set up there in his honor.

Finally, the "Archôn" (Henry) is represented as carrying the hopes of many thousands, "But chiefly of the Muse, and Martiall sprite." We have seen[44a] that two of the chief qualities most often associated with the prince were his patronage of literature and his favoring every kind of martial exploit.

The second "Vision," the one that concerns the palm tree, continues this theme. The singing birds are clearly the poets supported by Henry, melodiously rejoicing "in his deere aide, by whom they were upheld." We recall Peacham's own testimony in *"An Epicedium"*[45] where he speaks of Henry's arm "that held me up." Another note sounded in this second "Vision" is that of "uneasy lies the head that wears a crown." Peacham appears to have been particularly aware of the heavy responsibilities of kingship:

(For little wot we managing of Realmes,
The howerly cares and charge of Diadems.)[46]

One theme in the last "Vision" is certainly that some princes were fortunate "who never saw their raigne."[47]

The third "Vision" introduces the awful figure of Death. Here, once more, Peacham effectively adapts a convention. The other elegists had roundly berated Death for having taken Henry before his time.[47a] Our poet becomes a kind of *advocatus diaboli* for he defends Death. The effectiveness of his adaptation is due to his having made Death himself the mourner. It appears that the dart had miscarried:

Henrie the good, the great, unware I hit
With deadly dart before the timely day,
For at one neere him while I level'd it,
That sent more soules then I my selfe away,
Or feare, or fate the arrow did misguide
That he escap'd, and Noblest *Henry* di'd.[48]

When the poet emerges from the dreadful Wood he hears the charge:

When *Death* I heard accused every where,
As Theife and Traytor.

It is possible that Peacham recalled the innumerable diatribes against death. It was usual enough to assail death in elegies; it was unusual to assail it with the vigor of language used in Henry's case. The compliment is nicely turned at the end when the poet makes Death swear that it was "against his will" that the prince died: "For who knew *Henry* could not meane him ill."

In "Vision IV"[49] Peacham stresses two of the prince's characteristics, his ability to inspire respect and affection and his love of horses. The second stanza speaks of his being,

Ydrad of all for awfull Majestie,
Yet loving, and more loved lived none.

In the fifth stanza he presents Henry's charger in the funeral procession angrily stomping the ground for "His Riders losse,"[49a] an interesting extension of the pathetic fallacy. It is further extended in the fourth stanza where certain heraldic beasts representing various noble houses are introduced as mourners; and this device is amplified in the fifth "Vision"[50] where a whole menagerie of these heraldic animals are paraded. For Peacham's deep interest in crests and the like one has only to turn to *The Compleat Gentleman*[51] to find his long chapter on "The Practice of Blazonry." In the second stanza the picture he gives of Henry's outshining Phoebus "in his glorious armes" was a familiar one to the prince's audience. And the other picture in stanza six,

The fiery spirit whose aspiring flame
Brake out enkindled at his glorious light
Grew dimme and damp'd, as dying with the same,

may be compared with what some of the other elegists wrote, that all England was reduced with Henry's death.[51a] Peacham concludes the "Vision" with lines that are as close as he ever comes to hyperbole:

Oh let me never live I pray,
To feele the griefe of such another day.

The fifth "Vision,"[52] the longest, is the most philosophical. At the same time it is the most lyrical. Dr. Johnson might have found more leisure here for allusions and less for genuine grief. Certainly the reader brings away an impression that Peacham felt free to expatiate. Here we have a host of trappings, but ordinarily used with a kind of freshness. Here are elements of the pathetic fallacy,[53] which of course go back through Spenser even to Theocritus. Here are the *dramatis personae* of mythology, Orpheus, Philomel, Naiads, Dis, Neptune, Calliope, Venus, and Adonis.[54] Each serves its turn. But intermingled are some of Peacham's deepest philosophical convictions. His democracy shines clearly through:

> None for precedence strove, that they forgat,
> As ill befitting pensiveness of heart,
> But as they came in Loving league they sat,
> And each to each his sorrow did impart:
> For griefes doe grow by many bearers weake.

Even when he is most involved with the pathetic fallacy convention, he turns it into the channel of his thinking:

> If in a garden but the Mallow die,
> The Daisie, Dill, or Rose, it lives agen,
> And shooteth yeerely from his bed on high;
> But we endu'de with Reason who are men,
> Much fairer, stronger, if we once doe fall,
> No more on Earth our being have at all.

This does not fall so very far below the utterance of Othello over the prostrate Desdemona. One further impression one gets is that Peacham thought of his "Vision V" as something more of a unit. At the beginning he hears one singing like "Thracian Orpheus," and he swings back to him at the end:

> The Man, the Musicke, Bird, and Beast were gone,
> I left to mourne disconsolate alone.

Yet this does not mean that Peacham ever lost sight of his main objective. Sounding throughout are many of the notes struck by other elegists. For example, he allows himself the extravagance of saying,

> With *Dion* dead,
> All Musicke and our Merry daies are fled,

just as the others had implied England's days were over.[55] He must have been equally aware of the current notion that grief over

Henry's death was so great as to deprive poets of their power of expression:[55a]

> Much more he would have said but that with griefe,
> His voyce did faile.

In the sixth and last "Vision"[56] the first theme stressed is that the deceased are better off, a theme particularly emphasized in the Henry elegies. The poet is conducted to Elysium by "a lovely childe," his own Beatrice:

> It was *Elisium,* a delightfull plaine,
> Where *Zephyre* makes an everlasting Spring,
> And Fruits, and Flowers, doe all the yeere retaine
> Their tast and beauties, sweetest Birds doe sing
> In Laurell shades, where coolest silver brookes
> Divorce their courses by a thousand crookes.

The further theme is the Sophoclean one that men are lucky to have died young, the youngling princes, for instance, "who never saw their raigne." This, of course, is the whole argument of Spenser's Despair. It is in connection with these other young princes that Peacham shows his deep interest in history,[56a] an interest that goes back at least to his college days. He shows this deep interest in a series of learned notes.[57] Noteworthy is his introduction in the eighth stanza of the Black Prince, with whom Henry was compared. Following his practice of describing these historical figures almost like emblems, Peacham pictures him with "a Launce of wondrous length, preserved ever since." Inevitably, the tragic sons of Edward IV who were murdered in the Tower appear:

> A little lower sat two beauteous Impes
> Of smyling cheere, as fresh as flower in May:
> Not *Tyndaris* faire twinnes, *Pierian* Nimphes,
> Or *Myrrha's* Boy so lovely faire as they:
> These were the Brother-Princes that in bed
> The Tyrant slew and left unburied.

The note reads: "The lively pourtracture of these Princes came to my hands limned in a Manuscript which was written by *Anthony* Earle *Rivers* their Uncle, and given to King *Edward* the fourth; and this was the first booke that ever was Printed in England (as Master *Cambden* told me) this being the same that the Earle gave the King, bound in greene Velvet." In the next stanza "Prince *Arthur*" is introduced:

> . . . this, above an Orange flower,
> *Though seemes the fayrest, yet the fruit is sower.*

And the note: "Prince *Arthur* maried *Catharine,* Daughter of *Ferdinando* king of Spaine. By this device the Author seemes covertly to shew a distast of our Princes matching with Spaine." O his prophetic soul, when we think of what nearly happened to "hopefull Charles," mentioned by Peacham in the last stanza. In the end Henry is raised above all his predecessors, but only "by one degree."

For the "Visions" as a whole it may be said that Peacham, in spite of what some have said, was currying favor less than most of the other elegists. It may be said, further, that he was less extravagant in his adulation. This may be due to the interval between Henry's death and the appearance of *The Period,* but is more probably due to Peacham's characteristic moderation. We recall that he concluded *The Truth of Our Times* with a quotation from Hippocrates: "All things moderately, and in measure."

"An Epicedium"[58] follows immediately after the "Visions." The note's definition of the genre as "proper to the body while it is unburied" may account for the difference in quality between it and the "Visions." The poem gives the impression of having been beaten out in some haste. Many of the prince's same traits are stressed: Henry the warrior in armor, Henry "Loadstar of the Arts," Henry the navigator, Henry the Protestant, Henry who was taken young as punishment for "Earths all Horrid crimes."

Following "An Epicedium" comes "An Elegiacke *Epitaph* upon the untimely death of the hopefull Prince *Henrie.*"[59] Miss Pitman[60] quite rightly says that, in contrast to the "Visions," this poem reflects the mood of the seventeenth-century religious poets. In seven lines Peacham summarizes the prince's characteristics; their formal nature is shown by his making each line begin with "For," just as he had introduced each characteristic with "Farewell" in "An Epicedium." Here one does get the hyperbole that goes with formal writing. The usual themes, such as "For Griefe her selfe is stricken dumbe," are repeated, and there is heavy emphasis on Henry's being better off in Heaven. Clearly Peacham was reaching for the quintessence in a line like "For Love of Armes and Heavenly Arts." Perhaps the only stereoptic lines in the poem are the ones in which he expresses his contempt for hangers-on at court;[61] Henry is now, God be praised, where,

> Parasite, nor Spangled groome,
> With Courtiers vaine accloy thy roome.[62]

It is well known that Henry's favorite sister Elizabeth married the Count Palatine the year after Henry's death. From this union sprang in 1614 the young Prince Henry Frederick. In honor of the occasion, Peacham produced his poem with the gradiloquent title, *Prince Henrie Revived. Or A Poeme Upon The Birth, And In Honor of the Hopefull yong Prince Henrie Frederick, First Sonne and Heire apparant to the most Excellent Princes, Frederick Count Palatine of the Rhine, And the Mirrour of Ladies, Princesse Elizabeth, his Wife, only daughter to our Soveraigne James King of Great Brittaine* (1615). J. Payne Collier[63] calls it "one of the rarest of Peacham's productions, and a copy of it has never been publicly sold." Peacham precedes it with a dedicatory letter to the princess in which he expresses his gratitude to her for having taken "notice of me and my labours."[64] He goes on to say that he wrote the poem while he was spending time in the Low Countries with "my noble friend" Sir John Ogle, and he inscribes it "from Utrecht." He then addresses six Spenserian stanzas of high tribute to her. In these he protests that her brother's death had so overwhelmed him that he could write no more:[65]

> When laid my reedes for evermore away,
> To sleep in silence Isis' shades among.

The whole tenor is that with Henry's death, the Golden Age has passed:[66]

> Where are the Summers when the righteous Maid
> With ev'nest hand the heavenly Scale did wield,
> And golden deed with golden meed repaid?
> When Vertue was in price for Vertue held?
> When Honours daintie but desert did guild,
> And Poesie, in graces goodly seeme,
> Rais'd her high thought with straines that Nectar still'd?
> They are ascended with that glorious Queene,
> And she, alas! forgot, as she had never beene.

Peacham implies that with the new prince, the country may enjoy *Astraea redux*. And Peacham's own Muse is reawakened with this

> Royall child, who like another Sunne,
> From Rosie bed arised'st in the East.

The poet's great interest in pedigrees is evidenced when he traces Frederick's glorious descent and predicts a glowing future:

> Caesar, Henry, thou maist one day raigne,
> As good, as great, as ever Charles-maigne.

It is natural that the young prince should be made to inherit the qualities of his illustrious uncle, and should be born "To chase the Crescent from our Hemispheare."[67] The child was welcomed with unusual festivities:[68]

> When Piles bright burning, by the silent Moone
> In every street, of midnight made the noone.
> While silver bels, with iron tongues proclaime
> A new borne *Henry,* to the Nymphes of *Thame.*

Peacham then launches into what was perhaps his main theme, the education of the prince, a theme which he developed later in *The Compleat Gentleman* and the religious aspect of which he explored still later in *Thestylis Atrata:*[69]

> *Religion,* then first groundworke lay below
> Which inward though it lies, and makes least show,
> All other Vertues it doth strong sustaine,
> As weaker peeces resting on the maine;
> This shall his life establish and assure,
> Heighten content, and make his seat secure.

These "other Vertues" are specifically named: Temperance, Prudence, Justice, Clemency. Of the last two he writes, in a couplet that is not unworthy of Pope:[70]

> This crownes with Immortalitie his Fame,
> And sheds abroad, as Balme, his precious name.

There is significance also in his asking that Henry Frederick be taught "all good Learning, and to love the *Muse.*" When he praises two of the prince's predecessors, it is obvious that he hopes that Frederick will follow in their footsteps. The lines on Queen Elizabeth have the ring of sincerity:[71]

And shee, there shee, whom bleeding hearts inter,
Rather then those few stones at *Westminster:*
Whose name, even now my ravish'd sense doth pierce,
And with sweet Nectar sprinkeleth my verse,
Eliza Queene, the Maiden conqueresse,
Borne in triumphall Charriot, (I ghesse,
Like *Thomyre,* or that brave *Semiramis)*
From hundred handed *Gerions* defeat,
And his proud Castles fall in eightie eight.

The lines on James do not give the impression of being quite so disinterested:[72]

Thy Grandsire *James,* our Royall *Mercurie:*
Who with his wand all tumult caus'd to cease,
Fulfill'd our wishes, gave our daies their peace.

It was typical of Peacham to extend his lines, written for a particular occasion, to cover life as a whole;[73] it is the generic tendency in him. And so here:

The winged vessell is not by her helme
So much commanded, as a potent Realme
Is by her Princes life example lead
To frugall course, or vile unthriftihead.

He sums up:[74]

Oh heavens! to men yee give no worldly thing
More precious then the just and pious King.

He exhorts his countrymen to devote themselves to those just causes and to oppose with all their might the forces that work for evil in the world; let us, he says, turn from fighting each other to promoting truth, especially *religious* truth:[75]

If the easefull age your active spirits yrke,
Not weeting how to set your selves a worke,
Turne your keen steele against the hateful Turk.

One last factor that makes this poem distinctive is that Peacham uses the flower passage, not to weep for the dead but to rejoice with the living:[76]

The ripened graine shall yellow veile the ground
No serpent hurt, or harmefull hearbe be found;

Wood-Nymphes the shadie violets shall pull,
And bring thee Lillies by whole baskets full;
Some crop the Rose, to shew thee how in graine
That crimson Venus bleeding hand did staine;
How from that daintie daughter of the morne,
And silken leaves thy lovely selfe art borne;
Or Primrose, with the Kings enamell'd cup,
(Whose Nectar Phoebus early quaffeth up)
The Amaranth arraied in velvet still,
Sweet Rhododaphne and the Daffodill,
Soft Marjoram the young Ascanius' bed,
While Cupid kist and courted in his sted,
The frail Anemon, Hyacinthus soft,
The Ladies glove, Coronis weeping oft,
And whatsoever else the pleasant spring
Throwes from her bosom foremost flourishing.[77]

On March 28, 1624 Richard Sackville, fourth earl of Dorset, died. Peacham paid respects to his memory in *An Aprill Shower; Shed in abundance of Teares, For the Death And Incomparable Losse, of the Right Noble, Truly Religious, and Virtuous, Richard Sacvile, Baron of Buckhurst, and Earle of Dorset* (1624).[78] The earl was a grandson of the co-author of *Gorboduc*. Peacham had come to know him early in 1622.[79] The poem was dedicated to Anne, Countess Dowager of Dorset, and consists of an epitaph in Latin, a "Monument to the Reader,"[80] an elegy of 156 lines, two emblematical "visions," and an envoy. The elegy itself is written in decasyllabic couplets. It is clear that Peacham owed a great deal to the earl; the very household was a "Paradise to mee." In fact, he says[81] of the earl, "unto whom living I was more obliged then any other of his rancke in the Land." He goes on[82] to say that he never hoped to find anyone more "Bountifull to mee,"[83] or a "Patrone like to thee." To him Dorset was "great *Maecenas* of all Poesie."[84] With all such protestations we should take care not to accept literally what Peacham[85] says about his abandoning the profession of poetry:

Noblest Dorset, dead and gone,
My Muse with Poësie have done:
And in his Grave, now throwne thy Pen,
Sit downe and never rise agen.

After all, this was an accepted convention. Collier[86] quotes the passage from Camden, who writes that Spenser's "hearse was attended by the gentlemen of his faculty, who cast into his tomb some funeral elegies, and the pens with which they had been written." Similarly, in one of his Obsequies, Donne[87] said:

> Doe not, faire soule, this sacrifice refuse,
> That in thy grave I doe interre my Muse,
> Who, by my griefe, great as thy worth, being cast
> Behind hand, yet hath spoke, and spoke her last.

Peacham's deep gratitude to Dorset accounts for his overpraising[88] the lord's poetry. Henry King[89] speaks in the highest terms of his moral qualities and never so much as mentions his poetry. Peacham's extravagant praise also may stem partly from his having wished to please Dorset's widow:[90] "If ever Mortalitie clad true Honour, and Honestie of Heart, she veiled either in the Person of your Noble Lord and Husband."[91]

The fact that Peacham knew Dorset for a comparatively short time and, therefore, could regard him more objectively makes it plausible that he would have the lord stand for some of his own deepest convictions. The first was religion:[92]

> For, first his *Mind*
> Was best compos'd, Religiously inclin'd.

And Dorset could speak authoritatively in justification of his faith:[93]

> Whan
> H' entcountred *Papist,* or the *Puritan,*
> Who better vers'd in Scriptures and the Text,
> The Ancient Fathers, and our Writers next.

With religion went charity. It appears that the lord was constantly adding to the miserable pay which divines received, in Peacham's words,[94] "by adding Stipends to your Livings small." In fact, "From him Sad-hearted none return'd away."[95] He "fed The neighbour Poore, that else had famished."[96] These are exactly the same qualities he was to praise ten years later when writing his elegy on the Countess of Warwick. Dorset had not a vestige of the snob in him, was "Devoid of Pride, and haughtie-browed Disdayne";[97] he was "an enemie to garish Pride and Fashion, The Epilepsie of our English Nation." The strong language which Peacham uses here makes one aware of how often he must have suffered from the opposite attitude in many "nobles" of his time. We know from what he says about extravagance of dress in *The Truth of Our Times* that he admired Dorset's simplicity:[98]

> For with the plainest plaine, yee saw him goe
> In Civill blacke of Rash, of Serge.

Here both Peacham and Dorset stand with the Puritans rather than with the Cavaliers.

After the elegy comes "A double Vision upon the Death of this Noble Lord." These two visions resemble in some respects the ones in *The Period of Mourning*. They are written in rhyme royal. Significantly, the first vision is of a lovely Nymph who obviously represents the Church, and who is bewailing the loss of her staunch supporter:[99]

> To whom, ah whom, shall now I make my mone?
> Or who (shee said) will pitie my distresse?
> Sith now my nearest dearest Friend is gone,
> Who shall *Religion* (wel-nie Comfortlesse)
> Commiserate? (yet many doe professe
> A seeming friendship) and her labours cherish,
> Or give me Bread, that heere I may not perish?

That fillip within the parentheses is just as characteristic as the rest; Peacham had observed too many instances of religious hypocrisy. The second vision[100] is concerned mainly with Dorset's poetry and his patronage of poetry. The poet beholds "a goodly Lawrell" in whose protective branches the Muses delighted to sing. Then, for some reason which is never explained, the owner comes and ruthlessly cuts the tree down:

> That much my heart was grieved at the sight,
> But more, because the Muse had lost her Freind
> Whose armes from harmes her state did still defend.[101]

The tone of *Thestylis Atrata* is quite different. Whether he knew the Countess of Warwick well or not,[102] he succeeds in conveying the impression of a personal relationship. This was due in part to her ladyship's happening to share so many of Peacham's inner convictions. In other words, instead of the subject's being made to stand for those convictions, as was the case with Lord Dorset,

Peacham saw those same convictions objectified in the person of the countess. In any case, the countess comes through as a person, as the good Earl did not.

The Countess of Warwick died in June of 1634. Peacham wrote his tribute to her "shortly after her death": *Thestylis Atrata: or A Funeral Elegie upon the Death of the Right Honourable, most religious and noble Lady, Frances, Late Countesse of Warwick.* (1634).[103] The work is dedicated to her three nephews, the Wray brothers. Peacham protests[104] that he has been stirred by the sad event to raise up "my dead and forgotten Muse" because his debt to the countess was so great. He speaks openly of the "many favors I formerly received from her Honour." And again in the dedication[105] he insists "that my selfe have beene much bounden unto her, for her Honourable respect ever towards mee." He then goes into some detail about the nature of their relationship. It appears that "some few yeares agoe" her ladyship sent to ask his advice about the erection of a monument in Snarford Church. He complied by drawing a model for her, adding "a plaine, but short and proper Inscription, leaving underneath a space for an Epitaph, there to be inserted after her death." Thereupon, she commissioned him to write such an epitaph, and he agreed to do so.

Throughout the elegy the countess' essential goodness is emphasized. In fact, he mentions[106] "her Pietie and Goodnesse" and the "sweet humilitie of her minde." This goodness was so diffused in the neighborhood that the whole countryside suffered from her death:[107] "Townes and Tenants well-nigh undone are." One feature that makes the poem distinctive is that Peacham, often between the lines of poetry, runs a whole series of historical explanations in prose.[108] In "To the Reader" he justifies the introduction of many of the great figures of the lady's own county, Lincolnshire, by claiming to have "example of the best approved Poets." What he actually succeeds in doing is giving the impression that these great and noble persons somehow reflect their glory on the countess herself. Among them was her ladyship's own father,[109] "the Honourable Sir *Christopher Wray* Knight, Lord chiefe Justice of the Common Pleas," who contributed generously to Magdalene College, Cambridge,[110] and in return, "She [the college] weares his Armes and liverie on her gate."

With the Countess the first element stressed is her careful education. She was instructed,[111]

. . . in everie Science that was rare,
And commendable Art, that might concerne,
Or suited with Nobilitie to learne.

As we might expect, religion takes precedence:

But first *Religion,* they the ground-work laid,
Whereon as *Basis* all the other staid;
And hence that goodly structure of her minde
Proceeded, wherein with more state she shin'd,
And glorious lustre, than in that array
Of gold and jewels on her wedding day.
Her greatnesse, first of all she taught to know,
It was the greater while it kept below;
Pyramid-like the higher reared up,
The lesse it seem'd, and waxed at the top:
No over-weening scorne her brow did cloud,
Additament of honour made her proud,
That well she might that Royall *Motto* claime
Of great *Eliza, Evermore the same.*

Peacham has scarcely finished talking of her distinguished ancestry[112] when he dismisses these matters as of no consequence:

it is not Bloud,
Alliance, Honours, Fortunes make us good.[113]

It is rather, "Of her owne selfe, how great, how good was shee." He praises her that,

The Court and Citie seld frequented she,
Where all brave Dames and Beauties love to be.

And he vents his strong feelings against the pretentious status-seekers who are forever running up to London to observe fashions:[114]

Now blush (yee Dames) who leave your Mansions faire,
The fragrant fields, the healthfull Countrey aire,
Your walks, your woods, your flowrie gardens sweet,
To live immur'd within a stinking street,

. . . .

Or learne what fashion most is in request,
How is this Countesse, that Court Ladie drest;

While yee, your beauteous faces so disguise,
We neither see your foreheads, nor your eyes:
(Like Dutch Boores houses, where the straw hangs over
The low-thatcht eaves, and doth the windowes cover).

The countess, on the other hand, had sense enough to stay in "her owne faire Snarford" where the latch string was always out,

. . . keeping open dore
To neighbours, strangers, and the needie poore.

Her charity was well known, not merely in her immediate neighborhood but far and wide in Lincolnshire:

Her care of orphans, widdowes, whom she fed,
She cloath'd, and in their sicknesse nourished.[115]

She visited her tenants and talked with them as equals:

Her favour to her Tenants round about,
Of whom she never turned any out,
Or rais'd their rents, or failing at their day,
Tooke re-possession: no, she tooke their pay,
As they could best provide it for her, then,
Perhaps, if need, gave something back agen.

How much her charity was a by-word is shown in the poet's lines:[116]

I need not here relate (so knowne to all)
Her bountie *Raison* to thine Hospitall.

It was natural for Peacham to specify her benefactions to his alma mater; in a marginal note he says that "she gave exhibition to many Schollers in the Universitie of Cambridge." She even concerned herself with the welfare of prisoners:

And (like her Maker) she did heare the crie
Of poorest prisoners, that condemn'd did lie.
When on these waters she did cast her bread,
And even their soules at her owne charges fed.

Peacham explains this last allusion in the margin: "She allowed twentie pounds a yeare to a Preacher, to preach unto the prisoners at Lincolne." And it was often for the preachers she was most sorry, supplementing their miserable livings from her own resources:

Where Preachers wanted (as alas they want)
Were livings small, and their allowance scant;
Her Honour bounteous stipends did afford
To painfull Teachers of the Sacred Word:
Nor did she this in places one or two,
For her owne glorie, (as be some that doe)
But wheresoever she of want did heare;
(No matter where) within, without the Shire.

He shows how individual he wishes to make the portrait by adding in the margins: "Shee allowed twentie pounds yearely to a Preacher at Welton, a towne by her. Also twentie pounds yearely toward a Sermon in Ancaster."

But it was not like Peacham to restrict himself to the individual. He was forever reaching out to draw general conclusions on the basis of the individual's experience. And it is here that we learn more about his philosophy:[117]

She buried not her Treasure in a box,
And that againe enclos'd with sundrie locks
From theevish hands, but up to Heaven before
She sent it, borne by prayers of the poore:
She knew how here from basest covetise,
All evils, with contempt of God arise:
With love of riches who intangled are,
Doe easly fall into the Tempters snare;
How poyson in this *Idoll* Gold doth lie,
That take away the life of *Charitie;*
Parts father and the childe, then sets the mother
At odds with husband, daughter with the brother.
Yet did she nought profusedly bestow
For ostentation, or a trumpet blow
When she gave almes, but ever did impart
Them secretly to need, or due desert.

In the same way Peacham draws the contrast between the countess and the pretentious ladies whose sole objective was social position, and who in their ardent pursuit were totally unaware of the great leveler:[118]

See (Ladies) what it is that make you proud,
A verie nothing, an Ixions cloud,

When most belov'd, pursu'd, embrac'd and kist,
Dissolves it selfe to vapor and to mist:
A blushfull blossome, pleasing to the eye,
No sooner blowne, but blasted by and by.

. . . .

And Ladies see, that commonly contend
For highest place at Church, or Tables end;
How quickly can this enemie of life
Decide the quarrell, and compound your strife.

The inevitable conclusion is that,[119]

We follow fast as Pilgrims, thou dost die
Even reading this, and writing so doe I.[120]
How *vaine a thing,* alas, *is wretched man?*
By holy Scripture termed well *a span,*
A *Leafe,* a *Bubble, Froth,* the *Downe* that *flies,*
A wasting *Vapor, Smoake,* a *Cloud* in skies,
A *Post* that hasting makes not any stay,
A *Shadow* swiftly vanishing away,
A *Ship* that no impression leaves behinde
Where it hath past, a *Morning Dreame,* a *Wind,*
Hay, Grasse, a *Flower* (from whose faire golden cup,
The early Sun doth pearly Nectar sup,
Upbraiding with her blush the crimson morne,
But ere the evening downe with sith is shorne)
A *Bird,* an *Arrow,* and a *Shepherds tent,*
A *Weevers web* cut off, a *Vestiment,*
Snow water that dissolveth with a drought,
A short told *Tale,* a *Candle quickly out.*
That we no sooner from our mothers womb
Do draw this aire, but hasten to our tomb:
The *Rich,* the *Poore,* the *Little* and the *Great,*
Unlearned, Learned, Wise and *wanting wit,*
Death keepes no rank, or will be woo'd to stay,
Brookes no *excuse,* intreatie, or delay,
For *Age,* ne *Sex* he careth, all is one,
They as all Waters to their *Seas* must run.

He goes from praising the great beauty of the countess in her youth to the thought of beauty in general:[121]

Sweet Beautie, why art thou so transitorie?
Who with Ambrosian dainties feed'st our eyes,
And with our soules so neere dost sympathize:
Leading all captives, whom thy power encloses,
In hands of burnisht gold, and chaines of Roses.

Peacham then assails the Heavens for having allowed that fell sergeant, Death, to be so strict in his arrest. On second thought, he takes it back, conceding that "it was old Adams fault, his foule amisse" that brought death into the world:

There is no Royall bloud, or Noble race,
But must arise, and give his greatnesse place.
Death's King of *Heraulds* overlooking tombs,
At Church all placing in their proper roomes,
All marshalling at Funerals and Feasts,
Ranking with all equalitie his guests.

The man who has feasted on the goods of this world hates even the sight of a skull's head painted on the wall which he passes:[122]

But to the man who liveth in distresse,
In Want, in Prison, friend and fatherlesse,
To age, that wearie of the world doth see,
From bad to worse how times declining bee,
To bed-read, and the long tormented sick,
How happie is thy welcome, Death, how quick
Doe they embrace thee, as the wearie guest
Cals for his Host, and first would be at rest.

As he thus customarily passes from the individual instance to a general conclusion, Peacham just as customarily, to give his poem a sense of unity, swings from the general back to his subject. No pain or torment could make the countess solicit death:[123]

And when she saw the fatall houre draw nie,
She should be seene no more of living eye,
About her she her dearest friends doth call,
Advise and comfort all she can, withall
Blesseth her servants, wils them not to weepe
For her, who shortly in the Lord must sleepe,
And resting, her eternall Sabbath keepe:

On toilsome earth no more, no more with them,
But in the Court of new *Hierusalem.*
To mutuall love exhorts them, and to trace
The paths of *Vertue,* in their lives short race.

Our last view of the countess gives the impression almost of being taken from some relative who was actually present at her death:

Even as the *Hiacynth* doth change the hue,
Which (from the tender stalk where late it grew)
Some Virgins daintie finger off hath torne,
And that sweet tincture which it did adorne,
Not fully faded, by degrees doth dye,
Where some small remnant still affects the eye:
Even so a colour livelesse doth she keepe,
And lovely seemes, as one but fast asleep.[124]

Peacham concludes his poem conventionally enough by imagining the countess in heaven, sending down her injunctions and bidding her survivors not to mourn for her in her present abode where she is far happier than she had ever been on earth.[125] Actually, this is one element in unifying the elegy because Peacham had begun with an address to her in "Heavens glorious Palace."

EPILOGUE

In many ways Henry Peacham, Jr. is typical of the century in which he lived. He was still strongly under the spell of the Renaissance. But the kind of emphasis he placed on religion resembled more that of some of his contemporaries. He was proud to be an Englishman with its tradition of fine old aristocratic families. Yet he firmly believed that a "gentleman" had to be one in both senses. *Noblesse oblige* was a cornerstone in his philosophic structure. If a man was born to nobility, he had to prove his right to stay there. Politically, Peacham was a monarchist; but he was a staunch independent by nature, and sympathized with that class of society that, through its own efforts, was gradually improving its status. Many of his educational theories were traditional. But no one was more resolutely convinced that education must be adapted to the age. He followed Bacon in writing essays, yet the tone of those essays tended often to be Addisonian. Some of his prose works such as *The Worth of a Penny, Meum and Tuum,* and *The Art of Living in London* appear to combine features of the realistic "novel," as written by Dekker, Nashe, and Deloney, with elements of Defoe, Sterne, and even Fielding. He wrote satire, but it lacked the bitterness that Swift and Pope were to inject into the genre. Thus, if we regard the seventeenth century as the transitional one it is, we would look long to find a better example of that transition.

The impression I should least wish to leave with the reader is that Peacham was a man without firm convictions. For all his versatility, if he were to sit down to a crust of bread with Goldsmith or to a banquet with Dean Swift, neither of those estimable worthies would have the slightest doubt, by the end of the meal, just where he stood on fundamental issues.

APPENDIX

It has been mentioned above that as a background for the Countess of Warwick in *Thestylis Atrata* Peacham introduces a host of the famous men of her county, Lincolnshire, and adds prose elucidations set within the text itself. We are made aware once more of his deep interest in history. Since I have not seen these passages reproduced elsewhere, I will therefore give some of them here as being of interest, especially interesting because often they are statements by Peacham's contemporaries or near contemporaries about important historical events.

> Lincolne anciently by *Bede* and others called *Lindecollinum* (from the situation upon the top of an hill,) and also *Lindum,* whence that part of the Shire beyond the River of *Witham* was called *Lindeseia,* or *Lindsey.* By the Normans it was called *Nicol-shire,* by a Metathesis or transposition of a letter, as wee finde in a certaine deed made by *John of Gaunt,* beginning thus: *Jehan filz du Roy d'Engleterre, Duc de Guyenne, et de Lancastre, Conte de Derby, de Nicol, et Leycestre, Seneschal d'Engleterre* (sig. B 1 verso).

In the text Peacham refers to,

> that religious King of Mercia, who
> Here kept his Court eight hundred yeares agoe.

And in the note:

> *Offa King of Mercia,* who kept his Court in the Castle of Stallingburgh, in the Countie of Lincolne, now being part of the inheritance of that Noble and right worthy Gentle-man, Sir

> *Edward Aiscough* Knight: here also was Saint *Erkenwald* (sometime Bishop of London) borne, as I was informed by Master *Linall,* a great Searcher of Antiquities in this Countie (sig. B 1 verso-B 2.).

The last part gives us some insight into the way Peacham collected his historical information.

The text has "Great *Bollingbrooke,* the son of *John of Gaunt,*" and the note illustrates Peacham's interest in pedigrees:

> *Henrie Plantagenet* (who was *Henrie* the fourth) borne at *Bollingbrooke* in Lincolnshire, son and heire of John of *Gaunt,* by *Blanch* daughter and co-heire of *Henrie,* the first Duke of Lancaster, who tooke to wife *Marie,* daughter, and one of the two heires of *Humphrey* de *Bohun,* Earle of *Hereford, Essex,* and *Northhampton,* and Constable of England. He lieth buried by *Marie* his wife, in the Monasterie of *Christs* Church in *Cantuarburie,* under a pillar in the North Ile. To this Church King *Henrie,* with *Thomas Arundell,* Arch-Bishop of *Cantuarburie,* were great benefactors: he died, *Anno* 1412 (sig. B 2).

Text:

> Then that brave Worthy, *Willoughbie* the Great,
> Who wily *Parma,* did so soundly beat
> From *Bergen,* with his ever honour'd Son,
> Earle *Lindsey* living, lov'd of everie one.

Note:

> It was in the yeare 1588. *Parma* lying before *Bergen* two whole moneths together, was beaten thence by the valour of the L. *Willoughbie* Governour, Sir *William Drurie,* Colonell *Morgan,* and many other resolute and brave Commanders being then in the Towne, at what time were knighted for their valour, Sir *Francis Vere,* Sir *Thomas Knolles,* Sir *Nicholas Parker,* and Sir *John Poolie* (sig. B 2).

Text:

> Thrice-Noble *Sheffield,* the surviving glorie
> Of Eightie eight, and subject of that storie,
> When thy enraged thunder-belching *Beare*
> *Spaines* floting Castles did to peeces teare.

Note:

> The L. *Sheffield* Baron of Butterwick, and Earle of Mowgrave, who to his great praise and honour did notable service in Eightie eight, in that famous fight with the Spanish Armado, being then Captaine of the *White Beare,* one of her Majesties ships royall (sig. B 2-B 2 verso).

Text:

> With *Pelhams* also father and the son,
> Whose fear'd black lances their great honour won,
> When th'row the heart of *Belgia* they ran,
> Conducted by the silver *Pellican.*

Note:

> Sir *William Pelham,* who being at that time Generall of the Horse, over-ran (saith *Cambden*) all Brabant, *Anno* 1586. As he was an absolute Souldier, so his son was also a great Souldier and Scholler, as any Gentleman in the Shire, having left behind him a sufficient testimonie hereof; whose son is Sir *William Pelham* (a verie worthy and noble Gentleman) now living, of Brocklesbie in Lincolnshire (sig. B 2 verso).

The reference to the younger Pelham's being "now living" is a device often practiced by Peacham to bring the events right down to the present day. The reference to the "silver *Pellican*" is to the Pelham crest, another of his interests.

Text:

> And expert *Ogle,* able to command
> A *Xerxes* Armie, if that need should stand.

Note:

> Sir *John Ogle* borne at *Pinchbeck* in Holland, a verie honourable Gentleman, and my especiall friend, with whom I lived in *Utrecht,* when he was L. Governour thereof, whom (as well for Honours sake, as his owne especiall deserts, having done great service to the States in the Netherlands) I could not but (in this place) remember (sig. B 2 verso).

For some reason he was always particularly proud of his association with Ogle. "His table," he wrote, "seemed many times a little Academy." For a few weeks he was in camp with a detachment of English soldiers in the service of Maurice of Nassau.

Text:

> With all-lamented *Burrough,* who did see
> Too late their errours, who attempted *Ref* [*sic*].

Note:

> Sir *John Burroughs* borne at Stow by *Gainesburgh* and slaine (being shot into the belly) before the Fort there (sig. B 2 verso).

Text:

> With *Harwood, Smith,* and numbers unnam'd here,
> All children of their mother Lincolnshire.

Note:

> Sir *Edward Harwood* borne at Bourne, and a Colonell in the Netherlands, slaine (as it was reported) before Mastrecht, hee was by his last will and testament a great benefactor to the towne of Bourne. Captaine *John Smith* borne at Alford in the Marsh of Lincolnshire, who served under the Prince of Transylvania, and made a great discoverie in the North parts *America* (sig. B 2 verso-B 3).

Text:

> The wisest *Burghley, Atlas* of our State,
> Our Englands *Palinure* (whose care of late
> In greatest stormes of danger, steer'd the helme,
> And sav'd from wreck our farre engaged Realme)
> His birth acknowledg'd unto fennie *Bourne,*
> Though *Stamford* holds his ashes and his urne.

Note:

> Sir *William Cecill* Knight, Lord Burghley, and Treasurer of England, was borne at *Bourne* in Lincolnshire, *Anno* 1521. His fathers name was *Richard Cecill,* one of the Ward-robe to King *Henrie* the eighth, of the house of *Alterynnis* in Wales, his mothers name was *Jane,* heire of the noble house of *Ekington,* and of the *Walcots:* Hee died 1598, and was buried at Saint *Martins* in *Stamford.* Of this ancient family of the *Walcots* is

Master *Anthony Wolcot* of Lincolne, my loving friend, discended (sig. B 3).

Text:

And honour'd *Henneage,* of that ancient race
Of Haynton, here take your deserved place,
So true a servant to *Elizabeth,*
And by King *James* even honour'd after death.

Note:

Sir *Thomas Henneage* Knight, borne in Lincolnshire, hee served Queene *Elizabeth* 35. yeares a privie Councellor, Vice-Chamberlaine and Chancellor of the Dutchie of Lancaster. Hee had onely one daughter *Elizabeth,* married to Sir *Moile Finch* of Eastwell in Kent, who brought him a great estate, who after her fathers death (in regard of his former deserts) was by King *James* created Viscountesse *Maidstone,* and Countesse of *Winchelsea:* He died October 17. *Anno.* 1595 and lyeth buried under a faire Monument, in the Quire of S. *Pauls* Church in London. Of this family was Sir *Robert de Henneage, tempore Henrici primi:* and since the time of *Edward* the third, *Anno regni eius* 16. they have continued Knights or Esquires, and in continuall succession Lords of *Haynton (John Henneage* Esquire, being at that time in possession thereof) unto Sir *George Henneage* now living, and Lord of *Haynton* (sig. B 3-B 3 verso).

Text:

The reverend *Whitguift, Cantuarburies* Grace,
Whose memorie shall never *Time* deface.

Note in margin: "*Borne* at Grimsbie" (sig. B 3 verso).

Text:

And *Fox,* who did so painfully compile
His *Martyrs,* breath'd first, *Boston,* in thy soile.

Note in margin: "*Borne in* Boston in the *Butcher Row, or Shambles there*" (sig. B 3 verso).

Text:

Now *Wainflet* borne at *Wainflet,* (who did found
And build that goodly Structure from the ground

Of *Magdalen* in *Oxford)* place we here,
A Benefactor unto all the Shire.

Note:

> *William* de *Wainflet,* sometimes Bishop of *Winchester:* His fathers name was *Patten,* and lyeth buried in *Wainflet* All-Saints, under a faire monument of Alabaster, erected at the charge of this Bishop his son, who in his Episcopall ornaments (with another brother, who by his habit seemeth to have beene a Deane or an Abbot,) support the pillow under their fathers head (sig. B 3 verso).

It is obvious that Peacham, following his habit, had studied the monument with some care. He says elsewhere that he spent much time going around to churches and collecting historical lore.

Then Peacham comes to the countess' own father:

And prudent *Wray,* chiefe Justice of our Land,
To whom the subject which we have in hand
Hath more relation, than unto the rest,
Far bee't thy bountie should be here supprest,
And that the Muse should so ingratefull bee,
As (with the chiefe) not to remember thee;
To whom our *Cambridge* is obliged more,
Than any other named heretofore:
For her faire *Magdalen,* enlarged so
By his great gift, which that the world may know
A *Wray* did raise her to a faire estate,
She weares his Armes and liverie on her gate.

Note:

> This College was first an Hostell of Monks, afterward repaired by the Prior of *Ely,* and the Abbot of *Ramsey* and *Walden,* and at length made a College by the Lord *Thomas Audley* Baron of *Walden,* and Lord Chancellor of *England,* and endowed it with possessions, *Anno* 1542. What he left undone, was finished by the Honourable Sir *Christopher Wray* Knight, Lord chiefe Justice of the Common Pleas, and father of this deceased Countesse (sig. B 4).

Peacham next introduces the lady's two distinguished husbands:

> St. Paul the first, who drew his pedigree
> From those of *France,* and bare their Armorie.
> To that great house of *Luxembourg* alli'd,
> And many a noble family beside:
> Next honour'd *Warwick,* who did with his name
> Impart his Honour, gave her halfe the same:
> A fitter better match there could not be,
> He was right noble, good, and so was she.

Without bothering to mention the Sidney connection, Peacham writes in his note:

> *Robert* Lord *Rich,* created Earle of *Warwick,* in the yeare 1618. *August* 6. His first wife was *Penelope,* daughter to *Walter* Earle of *Essex*; this Lady, widdow to Sir *George St. Paul,* was the second, hee died at his home in *Holborne, March* 24. 1618. and was buried at *Felsted* in *Essex* with his Ancestors (sig. B 4).

One last note should be mentioned. Much later in the poem Peacham is writing of how the sensual gourmand hates the very thought of death:

> He loathes the wall that Death is painted on,
> And trembles at his fleshlesse *Sceleton:*
> *Memento mori,* and the Day of *Doome,*
> That Master-peece of *Angelo* in *Rome*
> Do damp his spirit, and offend his eyne,
> He better likes the draughts of *Aretine.*

And in the margin he puts: "Michael Angelo *a famous painter, who wrought that excellent peece.*" Underneath he has, "Icones obscenae *Aretini*" (sig. C 3 verso).

NOTES

LIFE

1. "Studies in the Works of Henry Peacham" (hereafter cited as "Studies of Peacham"), a thesis submitted to London University in 1933. The rubbing is reproduced on p. 16. The lettering below is not so clear; Miss Pitman conjectures that it might read "Junii 21." The previously accepted date had been 1576. I am happy to acknowledge that in this chapter I have followed the outlines of Peacham's life as based on Miss Pitman's thorough researches.

2. Partial confirmation of the date of birth comes through Peacham's reference in *Coach and Sedan,* London (1636): "Queene *Elizabeth* . . . rode . . . to heare a Sermon, presently upon the victory obtained against the Spaniard in *Eightie-Eight.* . . when I remember (being then a Schoole-boy in *London,* about tenne yeeres of age) so many Spanish-Ensignes, in triumph were hung up, that the leades of the Church . . . seemed to be veild . . . with Gold, Silk, and Silver." Quoted by Pitman, "Studies of Peacham," p. 22.

3. *Minerva Britanna* (1612), emblem (hereafter cited as em.) 170.

4. *The Compleat Gentleman,* Oxford (1906), pp. 126–27.

5. He boasts of his ability to draw a map of any town "to geometricall proportion, as I did of Cambridge when I was of Trinity College, and a Junior Sophister." *The Compleat Gentleman* (1906), p. 126.

6. Pitman, "Studies of Peacham," p. 24.

7. *Graphicé,* London (1612), p. 157.

8. He dedicates to Layfield one of his emblems in *Minerva Britanna* (1612), em. 65.

9. *Coach and Sedan* (1636), p. E 2 verso. Miss Pitman, "Studies of Peacham," p. 26, reproduces both stories.

10. Pitman, "Studies of Peacham," p. 29.

11. Two in the British Museum and one in the Bodleian.

12. *Minerva Britanna* (1612), signature (hereafter cited as sig.) A 2.

13. *Graphicé,* p. 25.

14. In the greatly expanded version, *Graphicé,* which appeared in 1612. In that work (pp. 172, 173) he becomes more specific when he refers to "Christopher Collard (whose sonne my scholler is now of Magdalen College in Oxford)."

15. *Graphicé,* sig. A 2 verso.

16. His work concerned painting as well. It is important to note that, in the new chapter added to the 1634 edition of *The Compleat Gentleman,* Peacham makes a special mention of Rubens' visit to England. The visit had taken place between 1634 and the preceding edition. Noted by Pitman, "Studies of Peacham," pp. 61–62.

17. "Not only our Brittaine but Europe her selfe is obliged, for his [Cotton's] industry, cost, and care in collection of so many rare Manuscripts and other Monuments of venerable Antiquity, being of the same most free and communicative, to all men of learning and quality." *Compleat Gentleman* (1906), p. 197.

18. Pitman, "Studies of Peacham," pp. 42–43. Peacham is under suspicion—if it can be called that—with another gentleman; he addresses epigram (hereafter cited as ep.) 29 of *Thalia's Banquet,* London (1620), "To Thomas Knyvet," whose grandfather left him "a goodly Armory" with "an excellent furnished Library" and "very rare antiquities."

19. *The More the Merrier,* London (1608), sig. A 2 verso.

20. The only difference was in the title page.

21. See Chapter III, nn. 5 and 10 below.

22. He mentions Whitney in *Minerva Britanna* (1612), em. 172 as well as in "To the Reader," sig. A 3.

23. It should be recalled that Quarles' *Emblems* did not appear till 1635.

24. See also ems. 14 and 17 of *Minerva Britanna* (1612).

25. Ibid., sig. A 2.

26. Ibid., em. 14.

27. See treatment of *The Period of Mourning* at some length in Chapter VI below. The Bodleian copy with Malone's notes had been lent, for obvious reasons, to Heidelberg. I therefore was not able to read his notes.

28. Pitman conjectures reasonably that he left some time before March, 1614. "Studies of Peacham," p. 43.

29. *Compleat Gentleman* (1622), p. 231.

30. *Thestylis Atrata,* London (1634), sig. B 2 verso. See Appendix below.

31. Sir John had come to help Prince Maurice of Nassau in his campaign against Spinola.

32. "Thalia loquitur," *Thalia's Banquet,* London (1620), sig. A 3 verso.

33. Pitman says he was with the army at least from September 7 to October 9. "Studies of Peacham," p. 48.

34. *The Truth of Our Times* (1638), pp. 127–8 (hereafter cited as *Truth).* One has the impression that he seldom took more pleasure than from writing his chapter "Of Travaile." Previously in *Minerva Britanna* (1612), em. 37, he had asked the rhetorical question:

    For who's he, that's not ravisht with delight,
    Farre Countries, Courtes, and Cities, straung to see.

35. Other places he mentions are Leyden, Arnheim, and Antwerp. He did *not* get to Heidelberg, as the DNB article says. He informs the Princess in his Dedication to *Prince Henrie Revived,* London (1615) that, with the fighting, the ways thither were too dangerous.

36. One signatory to the Treaty was Milton's friend, "Henrie Wooton Knight, Ambassador extraordinary of his Maiestie of great Brittaine."

37. "To the Reader," *A Most True Relation of the Affaires of Cleve and Gulick,* London (1615).

37a. Cf. below, p. 101.

38. Pitman, "Studies of Peacham," pp. 41–42, gives the essentials of the story. Conceivably it was because Bacon did not choose to pursue the inquiry that Peacham addressed one of his emblems to him. Cf. below, p. 65.

39. If we are to take a reference in *The Valley of Varietie,* London (1638), literally, he spent part of that period in St. Martins-in-the-Fields in London. He speaks in that work (p. 130) of being given a nonflammable substance by an Arabian, "when I lived in Saint *Martins* Parish in the Fields, twentie yeares since."

40. Pitman, "Studies of Peacham," pp. 8–9, notes, from an examination of a British Museum ms. mentioned by Joseph Hunter, that Peacham may also have taught in "Heighington School in Washingborough parish co. Linc." There is no indication as to when he taught there, if he did so at all. On p. 51, Pitman reproduces a picture of the Wymondham school. It was used continuously in that capacity until World War I. It now serves as a public library.

41. *Thalia's Banquet,* ep. 30.

42. The work will be referred to often and quoted at length in the following chapters.

43. *General History of the Science and Practice of Music,* 5 vols., London (1776), III, p. 194.

44. Cf. below, p. 104.

45. *The Gentleman's Exercise* (alternate title for *Graphicé),* London (1612), p. 167.

46. They were almost exact contemporaries.

47. In *The Art of Drawing,* p. 64, he writes: "There are many good peeces els in divers other places . . . unto which being drawne by their own antiquitye, and [my] love of arte, I have in a manner gone on pilgrimage, neither as I though loosing my labour, since I can shew almost eight hundred severall ancient coates, which out of old and decaied windowes, I have entertained from the injury of rude hands and fowle weather." He goes on to prove his allegiance to alma mater by asserting that Kings College Chapel has the best glass work in England. Some significance may be attached to the fact that an important chapter on "Antiquities" was added to the 1634 edition of *The Compleat Gentleman.* Closely associated with antiquities was Heraldry (Blazonry), treated in the longest chapter of the book.

48. *Thalia's Banquet,* ep. 70.

49. See p. 83, n. 132 below. Pitman finds that his chapter "Of Musicke" in *The Compleat Gentleman* constitutes the first account of the early English and Italian composers. See also "Studies in the Works of Henry Peacham," *Bulletin of Historical Research,* XI, p. 191.

50. *Graphicé,* sig. A 2. In this same dedication Peacham writes proudly, "By profession I am a Scholler."

50a. Cf. below, pp. 39–40.

51. *Thestylis Atrata.* See Appendix and p. 107 below.

52. Quoted by Pitman, "Studies of Peacham," p. 64.

53. Quoted by Pitman, "Studies of Peacham," p. 60.

54. *Truth* (1638), p. 13.

55. *Valley of Varietie,* Dedication.

56. "Studies of Peacham," p. 60.

57. The will was presumably drawn soon after her husband's death in 1623.

58. Drawn in 1634.

59. *Truth* (1638), sig. A3-A3 verso.

60. In "To the Reader" he keeps insisting on "what I have known by mine owne experience."

61. In "To the Reader," *Cleve and Gulick.*

62. *Meum and Tuum,* p. 32.

63. Pitman, "Studies of Peacham," p. 63.

64. "The Epistle Dedicatory," *Coach and Sedan* (1636).

65. Malone 580 in Bodleian Library, Oxford.

66. I have tried to analyze the essential qualities of this work in my Introduction to the facsimile edition, Columbia University Press, (1942).

66a. Cf. below, p. 41.

67. Dr. Harold Levitt in his thesis (see n. 85 below) fills in the necessary background for Peacham's politico-religious pamphlets.

68. *The Duty of All True Subjects to Their King* (1639), p. 12 (hereafter cited as *Duty*).

69. Ibid., p. 22.

70. Ibid., p. 23.

71. Ibid., p. 2.

72. Ibid., p. 31.

73. Ibid., p. 33.

74. *A Dialogue Between The Crosse in Cheap, And Charing Crosse,* London (1641), sig. A 3 (hereafter cited as *Dialogue*).

75. Ibid., sig. A 2 verso.

76. An interesting local allusion since Boston is only a few miles from Peacham's Leverton.

77. Because of a possible misprint, the date of actual printing is in controversy. It was entered in the *Stationers Register,* April 20, 1641.

78. If one is to judge by the number of editions. Miss Pitman ("Studies of Peacham," pp. 302–6) in her Bibliography lists nine by 1704 as well as several

modern ones. Professor Gordon praises the book: "It would be hard to find its equal for wit, vigour, and keenness of observation." (See 1906 edition of *The Compleat Gentleman,* p. xxi.)

79. *The Worth of a Penny* (1677), p. 5.

80. Ibid., page 34.

81. *Square-Caps Turned Into Round-Heads,* London (1642), p. 5 (hereafter cited as *Square-Caps).*

82. Ibid., p. 6.

83. Ibid., p. 7.

84. Ibid., p. 8.

85. See his thesis, "The Political Writings of Henry Peacham," New York University, 1968, last section, pp. 5–7. One passage at least is practically word for word from Milton's reproduction in *Animadversions* (1641) of a sentence in Hall's *Defense.* Peacham did not, of course, know the nature of the adversary he was taking on in the first of these.

86. *A Paradox in the Praise of a Dunce,* London (1642), p. 1 (hereafter cited as *Paradox).*

87. If Peacham had been jealous by nature, he might have envied Burton in his snug berth at Christ Church.

88. *Paradox,* p. 5.

89. *Paradox,* p. 2.

THE EPIGRAM

1. See Professor John William Mackail's *Select Epigrams from the Greek Anthology,* London and New York (1906), pp. 1–2 (hereafter cited as *Select Epigrams*). One advantage of the Mackail version is that he prints the Greek and then gives a prose rendering in English at the bottom of each page.

2. Mackail's definition will do as well as any. See *Select Epigrams,* p. 4: "The epigram in its first intention may be described as a very short poem summing up as though in a memorial inscription what it is desired to make permanently memorable in a single action or situation. It must have the compression and conciseness of a real inscription, and in proportion to the smallness of its bulk must be highly finished, evenly balanced, simple, and lucid."

3. Herodotus and Thucydides used epigrams as historical evidence.

4. Mackail is here following mainly the progress of love in the various periods. See *Select Epigrams,* p. 32ff.

5. In a much later period the classically trained Walter Savage Landor wrote: "The dignity of a great poet is thought to be lowered by the writing of epigrams."

6. Jacobs' monumental edition appeared, with full paraphernalia, in thirteen volumes in 1794–1814. A convenient form to use is Frederick Dübner's edition of 1861–72, based on Jacobs but containing Hugo Grotius' Latin translations. A convenient modern edition is that by A.S.F. Gow in two volumes, Cambridge, England (1965). Volume I contains the Greek text; the much longer Volume II (in which Gow was assisted by D. L. Page) carries an elaborate Commentary.

7. Some idea of the abundant variety may be gained from Mackail's discussion, *Select Epigrams,* especially pp. 28–29.

8. Perhaps with the idea that alliteration is an *aide-mémoire,* one rendering reads, "Money to mortals becomes a madness." George Burges, ed., *The Greek Anthology,* London (1893), p. 137.

9. Cf. Mackail, *Select Epigrams,* pp. 86 and 420. Cf. *Oedipus at Colonus,* 1225–28. It is significant that Sophocles wrote these lines in his very old age.

10. Burges, *Greek Anthology,* p. 121. In a Hamlet-like contemplation of a skull, the poet writes in language that anticipates Gray:

    Now let it tell to mortals that, though full
    Of other hopes, they lead but to the grave. (p. 346)

11. See J. A. Symonds, *Studies of the Greek Poets,* trans. W. J. Cory, London (1902), pp. 292–3.

12. Cf. *Epitaphium Damonis,* l. 142, "cinis ater."

13. Mackail, *Select Epigrams,* p. 55, n. 1, cites *In Memoriam,* XXIII.

14. See Henry P. Dodd, ed., *The Epigrammatists,* London (1876), p. xxxii.

15. See Mackail, *Select Epigrams,* pp. 74–77.

16. *Anthology Palatine,* VII, 496. *Greek Anthology,* 5 vols., trans. W. R. Paton, London, Loeb Classical Library (1917–26). Unless otherwise stated, references will be to that edition.

17. In some ways the most pathetic of all these pieces is the one by Poseidippus:

    "Why, sailors, bury me so near the shore?
    The shipwreck'd mariner's sad grave should be
    Far from the echoing breakers; in their roar
    Shudd'ring I hear my fate." (Burges, *Greek Anthology,* p. 477.)

    Cf. also the epitaph by Asclepiades, *Greek Anthology,* II, p. 155.

18. This almost fanatic attachment to fatherland is ironically shown in an epigram ascribed to Anacreon, who presents a youth so eager to see home that, against all warnings, he sailed in a winter storm and was drowned. Burges, *Greek Anthology,* p. 423.

19. *Greek Anthology,* II, p. 145.

20. Ibid., II, pp. 103–5.

21. Ibid., II, p. 379. The epitaph is one by Antipater of Sidon. Cf. also, "Sweet maid, thy parents fondly thought to strew thy bride bed, not thy bier" in Burges, *Greek Anthology,* p. 355. Cf. the Queen over the grave of Ophelia, "I thought thy bride-bed to have decked, sweet maid, and not have strew'd thy grave." *Hamlet,* V, i, 268–69.

22. Cf. Burges, *Greek Anthology,* p. 343.

23. Ibid., p. 472. Perhaps the prose translation conveys better the sense of the Greek: "My breasts labour for Hades."

24. *Greek Anthology,* II, p. 257.

25. Ibid., I, p. 165.

26. Ibid., I, p. 169.

27. Burges, *Greek Anthology,* p. 500.

28. *Greek Anthology,* IV, p. 97.

29. Burges, *Greek Anthology,* p. 469.

30. Ibid., p. 352.

31. Ibid., pp. 276–77.

32. Mackail, *Select Epigrams,* pp. 32–38.

33. In the seventy-six epigrams chosen by Mackail in his section on "Love," half are by Meleager. See Mackail, *Select Epigrams,* pp. 96–128.

34. Burges, *Greek Anthology,* p. 216.

35. Ibid., p. 483.

36. Ibid., p. 207.

37. Ibid., p. 234.

38. Ibid., p. 502.

39. Cf. the Chorus' great tribute in *Antigone,* 1. 331ff.

40. Burges, *Greek Anthology,* p. 108.

41. Mackail, *Select Epigrams,* p. 150. Simonides wrote an epitaph also on those who fell at Thermopylae.

42. *Anthology Palatine,* VII, 251.

43. Burges, *Greek Anthology,* p. 58.

44. Ibid., p. 127.

45. J. A. Symonds, *Studies of the Greek Poets,* pp. 340–1. The epigram is neatly turned. It speaks of the Persians having contemptuously brought a piece of marble out of which their sculptor was to carve a memorial to their victory; whereas Phidias used the same piece to celebrate the Greeks' triumph.

46. Burges, *Greek Anthology,* p. 440.

47. Ibid., p. 439. Not as fully established as Aeschylus'.

48. H. P. Dodd, *The Epigrammatists,* p. xv.

49. Burges, *Greek Anthology,* p. 346. Cf. pp. 310–11.

50. Ibid., p. 79. Cf. p. 309.

51. Ibid., p. 48.

52. Ibid., p. 201.

53. Ibid., p. 48.

54. *Greek Anthology,* III, p. 51. Cf. below, p. 30.

55. Burges, *Greek Anthology,* p. 202.

56. Ibid., p. 286.

57. Ibid., p. 315. This is another place where Herrick follows him.

58. Ibid., p. 430. The latter appeal is made by Simonides.

59. Ibid., p. 431.

60. Ibid., pp. 110, 288.

61. Ibid., p. 340.

62. Ninety of his epigrams are extant.

63. Mackail, *Select Epigrams*, pp. 69–70.

64. Ibid., p. 308.

65. Symonds, *Studies of the Greek Poets*, p. 306.

66. Burges, *Greek Anthology*, p. 440.

67. Mackail, *Select Epigrams*, p. 309. What might be Aeschylus' contribution is printed by Burges, *Greek Anthology*, p. 439.

68. Burges, *Greek Anthology*, p. 339. Inscribed on his tombstone.

69. Burges, *Greek Anthology*, p. 292.

70. Symonds, *Studies of the Greek Poets*, p. 302.

71. Cf. Burges, *Greek Anthology*, p. 347.

72. Ibid., p. 76. Cf. also Ion's tribute, ibid., p. 126. Jonson is thought to have followed Ion in his own tribute to Drayton; addressing the "pious marble":

    And when thy ruins shall disclaim
    To be the treasurer of his name,
    His name, that cannot fade, shall be
    An everlasting monument to thee.

    Some give the poem to Quarles.

73. *Greek Anthology*, II, p. 29.

74. According to Symonds' ascription.

75. Symonds, *Studies of the Greek Poets*, p. 302.

76. Burges, *Greek Anthology*, p. 229. It is possible that Plato is author of one neat tribute to him. See Mackail, *Select Epigrams*, p. 179.

77. Burges, *Greek Anthology*, p. 412.

78. Ibid., p. 22.

79. Ibid., p. 80.

80. Ibid., p. 287.

81. Symonds, *Studies of the Greek Poets*, p. 307.

82. Burges, *Greek Anthology*, p. 441.

83. With other Platos in the picture, Gow and Page appear to question whether any of the epigrams belong to the great philosopher.

84. Mackail, *Select Epigrams*, p. 415.

85. Ibid., p. 393.

86. Symonds, *Studies of the Greek Poets*, p. 293.

87. Burges, *Greek Anthology,* p. 15.

88. Ibid., p. 16. Lucian goes into detail about the Aphrodite of Praxiteles in Cnidos. See Symonds, *Studies of the Greek Poets,* p. 341.

88a. See above, p. 27.

89. Burges, *Greek Anthology,* p. 66.

90. Symonds, *Studies of the Greek Poets,* p. 334 and *Greek Anthology,* III, p. 79.

91. Burges, *Greek Anthology,* p. 332.

92. Cf. Symonds, *Studies of the Greek Poets,* pp. 290–92 and 339.

93. The misunderstanding appears to have taken its provenience in a typically foolish story which unfortunately has had some impact on serious criticism. See H. H. Hudson, *The Epigram in the English Renaissance,* Princeton (1947), pp. 6–7.

94. Meleager speaks of the epigrams of Callimachus as being full of "acid honey." See Mackail, *Select Epigrams,* p. 316.

95. Symonds, *Studies of the Greek Poets,* p. 314.

96. Burges, *Greek Anthology,* p. 61.

97. Mackail, *Select Epigrams,* p. 254. Lucian has a doctor who confesses that he is responsible for sending many souls to Hades. See Burges, *Greek Anthology,* p. 91. Martial says death could be caused just by *dreaming* of a doctor. See Andrew Amos, *Martial and the Moderns,* Cambridge, England (1858), p. 101.

98. Dodd's *Epigrammatists,* p. xviii. Also Burges, *Greek Anthology,* p. 501.

99. Mackail, *Select Epigrams,* p. 63.

100. Burges, *Greek Anthology,* p. 114.

101. Ibid., p. 388.

102. Ibid., pp. 33–34.

103. Ibid., p. 8. This is adder-tongued Nicarchus.

104. Ibid., pp. 492–3.

105. Cf. Mackail, *Select Epigrams,* p. 52.

106. Ibid., p. 52. Here the situation is summarized well: "The poor scholar had become proverbial; living in a garret where the very mice were starved, teaching the children of the middle classes for an uncertain pittance, glad to buy a dinner with a dedication, lecturing to empty benches or gradually petrifying in the monotony of the class-room."

107. Cf. Symonds, *Studies of the Greek Poets,* p. 311 and nn. 1 and 2.

108. *Greek Anthology,* II, p. 257. Mackail, *Select Epigrams,* pp. 86–87, quotes and cites other examples.

109. Burges, *Greek Anthology,* p. 169.

110. Ibid., p. 105. Cf. Lucilius (p. 106):

> Far happier are the dead, methinks, than they
> Who look for death, and fear it every day.

111. Ibid., p. 3.

112. Ibid., p. 167.

113. *Greek Anthology,* III, p. 89.

114. Ibid., IV, p. 183.

115. Lucian in Burges, *Greek Anthology,* p. 9. Ammianus more picturesquely says a man's beard is not the cause of wisdom but of lice (p. 35).

116. Ibid., p. 384. Ammianus.

117. Ibid., pp. 497–98.

118. A modern collection bears the significant title, *The British Martial: Or an Anthology of English Epigrams,* 2 vols., London (1806).

119. Because of the difference in nature of the last two books, some scholars reckon twelve.

120. One editor of an English translation (H.G.B., *The Epigrams of Martial,* London [1897], p. iv, hereafter cited as *Epigrams)* where he finds the poet to exceed the bounds of decency, prefers to use the *Italian translation* because, as he says, the French have gone beyond even the author "in his worst properties [*sic*]."

121. See Andrew Amos, *Martial and the Moderns,* p. 61.
For an adequate survey of Martial's characteristic uses of the epigram see T. K. Whipple, *Martial and the English Epigram from Sir Thomas Wyatt to Ben Jonson,* Berkeley, Calif. (1925), pp. 285–99.

122. This does not mean that he did not value the epic; in fact, he says *(Martial's Epigrams,* 2 vols., Cambridge, Mass. [1950], II, p. 239) he too would write an epic if he only had a Maecenas! He praises (*Epigrams,* p. 222) "the lofty epic of the sublime Virgil" and, when he appears to be writing condescendingly, he has in mind a poetaster like Statius. But there is some boyish glee in his saying that epics and tragedies may be praised while his epigrams are *read* Epigrams, p. 200).

123. *Epigrams,* p. 124.

124. He insists that what he writes does not represent his own morals.

125. See *Martial's Epigrams,* II, pp. 249, 211.

126. *Epigrams,* p. 298.

127. *Martial's Epigrams,* II, p. 13.

128. *Epigrams,* p. 253.

129. *Martial's Epigrams,* II, p. 251.

130. *Epigrams,* p. 244.

131. Ibid., p. 159.

132. Ibid., pp. 259–60.

133. Cf. ibid., p. 103. "I invited you, he says, for today, not tomorrow."

134. *Martial's Epigrams,* II, pp. 359–61; II, pp. 227–29.
This is to be seen also in the loving care with which he describes country houses near Rome. For instance, his account of Faustinus reminds us so much of Jonson's *Penshurst* as to make us think Ben was virtually paraphrasing. Here are all of the details of animal life on the farm, here are the natives coming in gratitude to bring their tribute to the lord, here are "tall

maidens, daughters of honest husbandmen" offering "their mothers' presents in baskets of osiers." The whole countryside is invited in, "nor does a stinted table reserve its dainties for the morrow, but every one eats his fill, and the well-fed attendant has no cause to envy the reeling guest." Here even is the same suggestion Jonson makes at his conclusion when he says that this is not merely a house but a *home*.

135. Amos, *Martial and the Moderns,* p. 69.

136. *Martial's Epigrams,* II, p. 169.

137. *Epigrams,* p. 49.

138. *Martial's Epigrams,* II, p. 225.

139. Ibid., II, p. 233.

140. Ibid., II, p. 331.

141. Ibid., II, pp. 317–19. Peacham had a similar period of barrenness during the ten years he spent in the country. Cf. above, p. 11.

142. Ibid., II, p. 343.

143. The Emperor was naturally flattered by these references to his foreign conquests.

144. *Martial's Epigrams,* II, p.325

145. *Epigrams,* p. 348.

146. Ibid., p. 57.

147. *Martial's Epigrams,* II, p. 233.

148. *Epigrams,* pp. 175, 343; *Martial's Epigrams,* II, p. 239, II, p. 145.

149. E.g., *Epigrams,* p. 342.

150. Ibid., p. 228.

151. Ibid., p. 83.

152. Ibid., p. 98.

153. *Epigrams,* p. 197.

154. In this respect also, Peacham followed him, though there were probably personal reasons for his doing so. Cf. below, pp. 44–45.

   Among those who quoted Martial most are Jeremy Taylor and the eighteenth-century essayists. In fact, one wonders what the latter would have done for their mottoes if it had not been for Martial.

PEACHAM AND THE EPIGRAM: MATTER

1. But in his estimate of the genre in general Peacham was undoubtedly aware that he followed Martial who, in addressing a rival, Tucca, asked "What lower style of poetry can I choose?" See Andrew Amos, *Martial and the Moderns,* p. 61.

2. Miss Pitman has conclusively proved that the poem is Peacham's. See Margaret C. Pitman, "The Epigrams of Henry Peacham and Henry Parrot," *MLR,* XXIX (1934), pp. 129–36.

3. *The More the Merrier,* A 3 verso. In another epigram (sig. E 1 verso, ep. 51) he compares his muse to a country woman.

4. Ibid., A 4. He speaks there of "these rude lines."

5. Ibid., sig. A 3—A 3 verso. Here he says that epigrams "in their natures are so crabbed." And in the same passage he speaks of "the rough Plane." In *Thalia's Banquet,* ep. 1, he refers to "these rude and ranker weedes" in lines that bear interesting analogy with the opening of *Lycidas.* And in epigram 19 of *The More the Merrier* he carefully puts the genre in its place:

   My Muse *Marullus* now severely blames,
   Good houres misspending in light Epigrams,
   Critick, her humor Ile for once excuse,
   She does but as your Citie wives doe use,
   About to entertaine a better ghest,
   Sweepe Cobwebs downe and get the chamber drest.

   It is of interest that he felt quite the other way about emblems. In the dedication to his own volume of emblems *(Minerva Britanna,* 1612, sig. A 2 verso) he speaks of the "ever esteemed excellencie of this kind of *Poesie."* And in *Thalia's Banquet* ep. 70, we are informed that he had projected "a second volume of Emblemes." In the same volume with *The Period of Mourning* (1613), sig. E 1 ff., occur four emblems. Prof. Ruth Wallerstein *(Studies in 17th-Century Poetic,* Madison, Wisconsin [1950], p. 75 ff.) has a long discussion of the emblem.

6. Thomas Bastard, for instance, says that "my booke [of Epigrams] is of the fashion." Quoted by T. K. Whipple, *Martial and the English Epigram,* p. 353.

7. In the margin opposite emblem 153 in *Minerva Britanna* (1612) occurs the following: "Ex Epigrammate . . . graeco vetusto."

8. As it happens, Salmasius' historic discovery of the Palatine manuscript coincided almost exactly with Peacham's first collection, *The More the Merrier* issued in 1608.

9. Sir Thomas More's and John Owen's were also well known.

10. The materials here are, of course, often taken from other authors, including King James himself, Rosemary Freeman, *English Emblem Books,* London (1948), pp. 74, and 79–80, finds that parts of *Basilicon Doron* derive from Caesar Ripa's *Iconologia* (1603). But the very fact that Peacham selected them meant that he must have set his approval upon them. It happens sometimes that the only difference between an emblem and an epigram is that the former is accompanied with a picture.

11. *Thalia's Banquet,* ep. 71. Peacham was an economical poet; he used practically the identical thing in *The More the Merrier.* See sig. D 2, ep. 37. This tendency to belittle his own work is often accompanied by his sense of humor as seen in *The More the Merrier,* ep. 59:

    My wit her fruite yeeldes like the Orenge tree,
    Som bloom'd, some green, some ripe, som rotten be.

    In *An Aprill Shower,* London (1624), p. 2, he writes:

    For by the *Genius* (which I hold Divine)
    Of each true Poet, (therefore none of mine).

12. *Minerva Britanna* (1612), em. 203. In em. 199 he says much the same, insisting that we should not respect family or wealth, but honorable actions.

Two of the people he admired most were the Earl of Dorset and the Countess of Warwick, and the quality he admired most in them was their democracy (see below, pp. 106, 109). Dorset, he emphasized, was "Devoid of Pride." In *Thalia's Banquet* (ep. 85) he has his fun at the expense of a man who boasts that his ancestry can be traced back to the Conquest.

13. *Thestylis Atrata,* sig. B 4 verso. Cf. below, p. 108.

14. *Minerva Britanna* (1612), em. 79.

15. *Thalia's Banquet,* ep. 47.

16. *Valley of Varietie,* p. 66.

16a. See above, p. 33.

17. *Minerva Britanna* (1612), em. 194.

18. He may, or may not, have been familiar with Palladas' thoughts on the subject:

> I am a poor man, but living in Freedom's company
> I turn my face away from wealth the scorner of poverty.

19. *Minerva Britanna* (1612), em. 179. He quotes Seneca.

20. Parmenio once wrote: "I know the freedom of a frugal feast."

In *The Worth of a Penny* (1677), p. 16, Peacham claimed that "any generous and true noble spirit, had rather . . . dine with my Lord Mayors Hounds in *Finsbury* Fields." In *Minerva Britanna* (1612), em. 94, he says he would rather be free "then eate some caterpillar's envied bread," or "at anothers curtesie be fed."

21. His declared independence of tradition is also to be seen in *Graphicé* where, in his address "To the Reader," he boasts that the rules he follows are his own, "the very same Nature acquainted me withall from a child."

22. This note of ingratitude was one he sounded from time to time as in *Minerva Britanna* (1612), em. 74.

> Ingratefull times and worthles age of ours,
> That lets us pine, when it hath cropt our flowers.

23. *Minerva Britanna* (1612), em. 120.

24. Ibid., em. 50.

25. *The More the Merrier,* sig. C 2, ep. 25.

26. *Minerva Britanna* (1612), em. 97.

In *A Paradox in the Praise of a Dunce,* p. 1, he proves to his own satisfaction that he is no dunce because he lacks preferment.

27. His general disillusionment with the age may be read in ep. 115 of *Thalia's Banquet* where he contends that learning wants reward in "this worst age of iron." And in *Thestylis Atrata,* sig. C 3 verso, he repeats, "from bad to worse how times declining bee."

28. *Minerva Britanna* (1612), em. 24. In em. 26 he pays one of his many tributes to learning.

29. Ibid., em. 200.

30. He reemphasizes this point in *Thestylis Atrata,* sig. A 3, where he speaks of "the disesteeme of Poetrie in this latter age of the world, (wherein, to scorne

learning, and to know nothing, are accounted gentlemanlike qualities)." In *Minerva,* em. 197, he says that love of money has throttled Minerva. This sense of the artist's not being appreciated went so far that he thought of abandoning poetry for more serious and profitable pursuits. His mood was such that he endorsed what an earlier epigrammatist had written. Francis Thynne's *Emblemes and Epigrames,* London (1876), p. 96, em. 76:

Then cease, thow wearie muse, allwaies to beate thy brayne
And weare thy paynefull hand, which never reaped gaine;
Since all thy sweating toyle finds but such hard event
As damned *Sisyphus,* most bitter punishment.

In *A Caution to Keepe Money* (alternate title for *The Worth of a Penny),* pp. 5–6, Peacham writes, "A Cobler shall have as much respect as a Scholler." When Martial protests that the very mule driver is better off than the poet (Martial's *Epigrams,* II, p. 213; cf. also ep. LXXIV on p. 211), he has chiefly in mind finances. And here too Peacham follows him in *The More the Merrier,* sig. D 3, ep. 41:

What cheare since come to town I aske my purse,
Like one new purgd, it answers, never worse.

Further, there is an element of Martial in his regretting that his economic position requires, in return for gracious hospitality, that he be forced to provide only "meane collation" *(Thalia's Banquet,* ep. 63).

31. *Minerva Britanna* (1612), em. 39. In his epigram addressed to Drayton *(Thalia's Banquet,* ep. 38) he deplores that there are few good patrons just for the reason that so few can understand poetry.

32. This other side of the coin should here be emphasized. In ep. 57 of *Thalia's Banquet* he has high praise for a patron of the arts, his "true friend." This man, refined by travel in France and Italy, knows how to value learning. In ep. 49 he acknowledges "my kind and learned friend." Then he goes on in ep. 55 to speak of another who was "the only favourer of the Muse," and in ep. 121 he pays warm tribute to still another friend who has obviously been of assistance to him. In this last case he sends the patron samples of his poetry. Martial was not above doing the same.

33. *Thalia's Banquet,* ep. 40. Cf. also ep. 22.

34. *Thalia's Banquet,* ep. 62.

In a single couplet (ep. 42) he pays high tribute to Sir John Heveningham:

If *Honesty* in any one place rest,
She, Sir, hath tane her loging in your brest.

35. Martial asks Bithynicus whether he wants to become rich; then become a panderer to vice, virtuous courses will get you nothing. *Epigrams,* p. 284, ep. 50.

36. *Thalia's Banquet,* ep. 79.

37. *Thestylis Atrata,* sig. B 4 verso. Cf. below, pp. 107–8.

38. He may be thinking of the Greek inscription: "Holiness is to have a pure mind." See Mackail, *Select Epigrams,* pp. 46 and 200, ep. 15.

39. In *Thalia's Banquet,* ep. 14, he goes so far as to question even the sanity of some Puritans.

In em. 171 in *Minerva Britanna* (1612) he carefully distinguishes between the moderate and extreme Puritan:

There is a sect, whome *Puritans* they call,
Whose pride this Figure fitteth best of all.
Not such I meane, as are of Faith sincere,
And to doe good endevour all they can,
Would all the world of their religion were,
We taxe th' aspiring factious Puritan:
Whose Paritie, doth worst confusion bring,
And Pride presumes to overlooke his King.

In the righthand margin opposite this passage (British Museum copy) someone has written in an old hand: "In this he shows his flattering Folly and atheism, as well as falshood." The writer left no doubt what faction he belonged to.

40. *The Worth of a Penny,* (1677), p. 25: "How healthful are Scholars in our *University,* whose commons are no more then needs must!"
And just below (p. 27): "We, the Apes of *Europe,* like *Proteus,* must change our shapes every year, nay, quarter, moneth and week."
He admired the Earl of Dorset because he dressed in "plainest plaine" "in Civill blacke of Rash, of Serge" (*Aprill Shower,* p. 3). See below, p. 106.

41. In that *omnium gatherum, The Valley of Varietie* (1638), p. 23, he does record "the Romish Idolatrie" and speaks of "the Popes Tyranny," giving high praise to the Reformation.

42. Cf. "No conquest doubtles, may with that compare, Of our effectes [emotions], when we the victors are" (*Minerva Britanna* [1612] em. 93).

43. Em. 11, also addressed to James, contains this patriotic strain. Throughout *Minerva Britanna,* Peacham pays court, not merely to James, but to Queen Anne, Prince Henry, Prince Charles, and Princess Elizabeth.
Martial had praised Nerva's poetry just as Peacham praised that of James.

44. *Minerva Britanna* (1612) em. 137.

45. Ibid., em. 171. In em. 160 he emphasizes a man's duty: "First God to serve, and afterwardes his Prince."

46. Ibid., em. 65. This is to his tutor, "Mr. D. Laifeild."

47. Ibid., em. 98. His debt is deep to the university,

Which first enflam'd to this, my duller spright,
And lent in darke, my Muse her candle light.

48. *Thalia's Banquet,* ep. 51. This is addressed to another Trinity Fellow, "Maister Sam Simson."

49. Ibid., ep. 56. To prove he was not narrowly academic, he praises Oxford at the same time, contending the two are equal to the best universities in the world and specifically naming Paris, Salamanca, and Coimbra in Portugal.

50. Ibid., ep. 80. He had said much the same thing in *The More the Merrier,* sig. D 1 verso, ep. 34. Similarly Martial, after giving a list of places famous for their authors, says he hopes Bilbilis will be proud of Licinianus and him. See *Epigrams of Martial,* p. 57, ep. 61. In another epigram *(Martial's Epigrams* [1950], II, p. 231) Martial reminds his townsmen that Verona owes no more to "elegant Catullus" than Bilbilis owes to him.

51. In passing, it is worth mentioning that Peacham, like Milton, writes his own *Ad Patrem* to Henry Senior, "of Leverton in Holland in the Countie of

Linc": the well-known author of *The Garden of Eloquence.* See *Minerva Britanna,* em. 170. In the two cases the father-son relationship had many similarities.

52. *Thalia's Banquet,* ep. 73.

53. *Thalia's Banquet,* ep. 30. Peacham held much in common with the Alexandrian Palladas, who sang eloquently the woes of the poverty-stricken schoolmaster. See *Greek Anthology,* III, p. 91 (bk. IX, ep. 174).

54. *Truth* (1638), p. 19.

55. Miss Pitman ("Studies of Peacham," p. 190) questions that he tutored abroad the sons of Thomas Howard, as has been assumed. The two elder were at most six and seven when Peacham took his continental journey in 1613–14, and the youngest was not even born.

56. *Truth* (1638), p. 20.

57. Ibid., p. 26.

58. *Thalia's Banquet,* ep. 70. He addresses another of his students, Hannibal Baskervile, in *Minerva Britanna* (1612), em. 106. Cf. also "To my ever loved scholler Maister *Hammond Claxton" (Thalia's Banquet,* ep. 104).

59. *Mutatis mutandis,* some lines in *Epitaphium Damonis* also bear resemblance to the above.

Epigram 87 of *Thalia's Banquet,* addressed to another pupil, John Cock of Deepham, who became an attorney, brings out Peacham's sense of humor:

> If *Reason* be the soule of *law,* I faine
> In this point (pupill) would resolved bee,
> How is it that a statute doth maintaine,
> That when the *law* defines the contrarie,
> Yet *reason,* though far stronger, must give place,
> And *law* against *reason* carry cleare the case.

Similarly he pokes good-natured fun at his former pupil Hammond Claxton, now a prosperous clothier in Cheapside. Hammond has asked him what favor he can do for past favors. Peacham replies that all he has to do is walk by Hammond's splendid shop in his shabby clothes and it will be obvious what can be done for him, See *Thalia's Banquet,* ep. 104:

> But let me *Hammond* go in quiet by,
> For thou knowst what I lacke as well as I.

Martial speaks of his own thread-bare clothes (*see Epigrams,* p. 115, ep. 58).

60. *The More the Merrier,* ep. 33, sig. C 4–C 4 V.

61. *The More the Merrier,* sig. D 1.

62. See, for example, *Epigrams,* pp. 570–1, ep. 57.

63. *Minerva Britanna* (1612), ems. 184 and 185. The latter is one of the longest (two and one-half pages) in the collection.

64. One cannot help wondering whether he was aware of Palladas's vicious attack:

> All wives are bad—yet two blest hours they give,
> When first they wed, and when they cease to live.
> (quoted in *The Epigrammatists,* p. xviii)

Peacham appears to have had several quarrels with the sex. First, they talk too much; in ep. 35 of *Thalia's Banquet* he says that three women are "as loud as if an hundred men did talke." Then, he cannot abide the managing woman (ep. 52). Neither is there any peace when a woman is around (ep. 110):

From *Norwich* e're since *Ello* had his wife,
He never led one minute quiet life.

She comes off no better in *The More the Merrier* (ep. 31): "She never lied but once, that's all this while." In ep. 14 of the same work he pillories a lazy woman who lies abed till noon.

At the same time we know that Peacham spoke in the highest and most sincere terms of individuals, such as the Countess of Warwick. For this reason one hesitates to call him a misogynist.

65. *Truth* (1638), p. 47.

65a. Cf. above, p. 12.

66. *Minerva Britanna* (1612), ep. 132.
On the other hand, this was probably written before his marriage. If so, he would be out of all patience with himself as having been forewarned.

67. *Thalia's Banquet,* ep. 82.

68. Ibid., ep. 45.

69. Ibid., ep. 112.

70. The editor of *The British Martial,* 2 vols., London (1806), has expressed it well: "There is something not *sterling* in most of their [French] epigrams; and they appear to me to labour more for unnatural *point* and *antithesis* than for beauty of thought and forcible expression." The French understood the Greek epigram as well as they understood what Aristotle meant by "unity."

71. *Thalia's Banquet,* ep. 13.

72. Ibid., ep. 20. See also ep. 53:

I use my dog as Courtiers do, quoth he,
Their followers: he getteth nought by guift,
I give him count'nance, and so let him shift.

72a. Cf. below, pp. 108–9.

73. *Thestylis Atrata,* sig. C 4. His contempt for courtiers in general is well expressed in *Minerva Britanna* (1612), em. 115, where he alludes to them as harpies, tale bearers, parasites, backbiters. Especially contemptible are the courtiers who "turn their halcyon beaks With every gale and vary of their masters." The extravagant overdressing clearly disturbed him as ep. 75 of *Minerva Britanna* (1612) shows:

Great Lordes, and Ladies, turne your cost and art,
From bodies pride, t'enritch your better part.

And he is especially hard on the "Courtly Dames" in ep. 116:

Why should ye then as slaves to loathed pride,
And frantique fooles, thinke ye are halfe undone,
When that ye goe not in your cullors pide,
Or want the grace, of newest fashion.

74. *Minerva Britanna* (1612), em. 198. Cf. em. 63.

the proude vaine-glorious wight,
Who where he comes, will make a goodly show
Of wit, or wealth, when it is nothing so.

In em. 205 he satirizes the man who changes his personality with every person he meets. The pretender is bitterly assailed in ep. 42 of *The More the Merrier.* His female counterpart, a country wench who had been lucky enough to marry wealth, looks down her nose at her former friends in ep. 52:

> Scorning her neighbours, countrey, and her kin,
> And eke the paile that she had milked in.

75. Lines in *Thalia's Banquet,* ep. 16, anticipate in part the famous conclusion of Temple's essay "Of Poetry":

> Rich men their wealth as children rattles keepe,
> When plaid a while with't, then they fall asleepe.

Temple was to write: "When all is done, human life is, at the greatest and the best, but like a froward child, that must be played with and humored a little to keep it quiet till it falls asleep."

76. *Minerva Britanna* (1612), em. 104.

77. *Minerva Britanna* (1612), ems. 121, 129.

78. *Thalia's Banquet,* ep. 72. Everard Guilpin in *Skialetheia* (1598) writes of the lord's lazy life in the same vein.

79. *Thalia's Banquet,* ep. 122.

80. *Minerva Britanna* (1612), em. 84. We should expect Peacham to have contempt for the hunting class; when at table a serious discussion is launched, young Alphonso of ep. 22 in *The More the Merrier* can't take part out of ignorance, "Or 's voice is lost with following his hounds."

81. *Thalia's Banquet,* ep. 43.

82. *The More the Merrier,* ep. 11.

83. *Thalia's Banquet,* ep. 115.

84. *Thalia's Banquet,* ep. 90. Even more demeaning are his strictures on "Lucius the lately knighted Farmers sonne," whose name is to be seen "in every whoore-house seeling ore your head," even "in *Hobsons* Waggon" *(The More the Merrier,* ep. 15). In ep. 42 Furius comes off no better by proving himself to be a "a vertuous Gentleman": "His *Valour's* knowne in every baudie house."

85. *Minerva Britanna* (1612), em. 157. He criticized the people of Holland where, he had observed, the custom was more honored in the breach than the observance *(Thalia's Banquet,* ep. 111). Cf. below, p. 62.

86. *Thalia's Banquet,* ep. 96.

87. Ibid., ep. 106.

88. Ibid., ep. 72.

89. *The More the Merrier,* ep. 13.

90. *Thalia's Banquet,* ep. 89. He calls the glutton Runcer "*Time* that doe's devoure all." *The More the Merrier,* ep. 48.

91. See *Epigrams,* pp. 48, ep. XLII and 285, ep. LIII.

92. *Thalia's Banquet,* ep. 24.

93. Ibid., ep. 2. Cf. also *The More the Merrier,* ep. 40.

94. *The More the Merrier,* ep. 27.

94a. See above, p. 20.

95. *Paradox,* p. 3.

96. Milton voiced the same strictures, about a minister who "huddled up" a sermon in some off-hour.

97. *Paradox,* p. 5.

98. *Thalia's Banquet,* ep. 11. Peacham appears to have liked this epigram for he repeats it in *Truth* (1638), p. 69. He attacks extravagant fashions in ep. 125 also. And in *Aprill Shower* (p. 3) he calls "garish Pride and Fashion" "the Epilepsie of our English Nation." He addresses a lady in *The More the Merrier,* ep. 21, as follows:

I knew thee not (I crie thee mercie) *Grace,*
In thy French bodie, and thy English face.

99. *The More the Merrier,* ep. 39. Guilpin and Turberville are similarly critical of women's painting themselves. See *Skialetheia* (1598), ep. 61, and *Epitaphes* (1567), 148.

100. *The More the Merrier,* ep. 6. In *Thestylis Atrata* he writes:

While yee, your beauteous faces so disguise
We neither see your foreheads, nor your eyes.

101. *Thalia's Banquet,* ep. 105.

102. In ep. 18 of *Thalia's Banquet* he had in the same way reflected on Gellia's teeth:

When school-girl, Gellia's teeth were like pearls.
After she ate sweets, they turned blue like opals.
Now that she takes tobacco they have turned to jet.

103. *The More the Merrier,* ep. 18. He singles out "blew-starch *Joan*" "that will do reason for a very litle."

104. *Thalia's Banquet,* ep. 113. It is significant that he chooses Paul's with which to compare his own variety of interests. See *The More the Merrier,* ep. 43.

105. *The More the Merrier,* ep. 29.

"Great Hattens tombe" would hardly escape Peacham's notice. See *Thalia's Banquet,* ep. 40.

106. *Truth* (1638), pp. 103–4. Referred to in *Truth,* ed. R. R. Cawley (1942), p. xiv.

107. *Thalia's Banquet,* ep. 94. Twelve years earlier in "To the Reader," sig. A 3, preceding *The More the Merrier,* he had said practically the same thing in prose.

108. *Thalia's Banquet,* ep. 112. The traveler pretends not to like Virginia "cause their aire is foggy." Some significance is to be attached to his having mentioned the colorful Coryat in the preceding epigram (111) because Peacham wrote three poems to precede *Coryat's Crudities.*

109. Ibid., ep. 83.

110. *The More the Merrier,* sig. B 1 verso.

111. Ibid., ep. 30.

Martial was pestered in the same way. See *Epigrams,* p. 149, ep. 44.

In *Thalia's Banquet,* ep. 9, Peacham writes "Upon Dare an upstart Poet." Martial is even harsher on poetasters. See *Epigrams,* p. 121, ep. LXXI. When he heard a poetaster's house had burned down, he facetiously expressed a hope that the "poet" had burned with it! See *Martial's Epigrams* II, p. 303, ep. XCIII.

PEACHAM AND THE EPIGRAM: MANNER

1. *The More the Merrier,* ep. 43.
2. Ibid., sig. A 2 verso. He signs this "Epistle" "from my lodging in Fetter-lane neere unto Fleetstreet, this 4. of Aprill."
3. *Thalia's Banquet,* ep. 127.
4. Ibid., "Thalia loquitur," sig. A 3 verso. It is noteworthy that the first to be welcomed are "Academicks all."
5. This line may possibly indicate that Peacham did not write this Prologue.
6. *Thalia's Banquet,* ep. 127.
7. *Minerva Britanna* (1612), em. 177. This emblem is headed "Henricus Peachamus." At the top is "Anagramma Nominis Authoris." Since no source is given in the margin, the assumption is that the whole is Peacham's.
8. *Thalia's Banquet,* ep. 1.
9. In the Introduction to his edition of *The Compleat Gentleman* (1906), p. x. Peacham also felt convinced that his poetry was not sufficiently appreciated. See above, pp. 39–40.
10. *The More the Merrier,* ep. 62. This is the last one in the collection.
11. We have already seen that Peacham has in the margin opposite em. 153 of *Minerva* the following: "ex Epigrammate . . . graeco vetusto."
12. *Greek Anthology,* III, p. 89, ep. 172. Cf. above, p. 33. Parmenio said much the same, "I hate senseless wealth," concluding "I know the freedom of a frugal feast." See *Greek Anthology,* Burges, p. 30.
13. Mackail, *Select Epigrams,* p. 52.
14. Burges, *Greek Anthology,* p. 137, ep. 191. "Money to mortals becomes a madness."
15. Ibid., p. 6.
16. See *The More the Merrier,* sig. C 4 verso:

    What pleasure more, Marcellus, can theere be?
    Then in thy Garden to behold in *May,*
    How manie flowers, what variety
    Are, while thou slept'st, shot forth since yesterday.

    He follows with a detailed list of sundry flowers with their properties, which shows almost a horticulturist's knowledge. Cf. *Minerva Britanna* (1612) em. 185.
17. *Martial's Epigrams,* II, p. 179, ep. 33.
18. *The More the Merrier,* sig. A 2 verso.
19. Ibid., sig. A 2 verso.
20. *Martial's Epigrams,* II, p. 383, ep. 94. Cf. *The More the Merrier,* sig. A 3 verso. See above, p. 37.
21. *Epigrams of Martial,* p. 221, ep. 2. Cf. *The More the Merrier,* ep. 45.

21a. See above, pp. 34–35.

21b. See above, p. 42.

22. *Epigrams,* p. 57, ep. 61. See above, p. 42, n. 50. Cf. also *Martial's Epigrams,* II, pp. 231–2, where he boasts, "I am your glory and repute."

23. *The More the Merrier,* sig. D1 verso, ep. 34. See above, p. 42.

24. See *Epigrams,* pp. 104–5 and pp. 492–93, ep. 90. Cf. above, p. 44, n. 64.

25. Cf. Chapter III, above, n. 64.

26. *Epigrams,* p. 311, ep. 16, and p. 355, ep. 14.

27. *The More the Merrier,* sig. D 3, ep. 41.

28. *Epigrams,* p. 284, ep. 50.

29. Cf. above, p. 39, n. 30.

30. *Epigrams,* ep. 484, ep. 74.

30a. *Epigrams,* p. 124, ep. 77.

31. *Thalia's Banquet,* ep. 9.

32. Cf. *Greek Anthology,* ed. Burges, pp. 123–4, 351, 423, 477. Cf. also Mackail, *Select Epigrams,* pp. 74–75.

33. One wonders to what extent this might be extended to poetry of the first half of the seventeenth century as a whole. Thus, William Cartwright's "To the Memory of a Shipwrackt Virgin" might be regarded as something of an exception.

34. Mackail, *Select Epigrams,* pp. 322 and 35–37.

35. Ibid., p. 32 ff.

    On the other hand, love is clearly not absent from the *Anthology.* See ibid., pp. 143 ff., 204 ff., 250 ff. Some make the point that love did not come prominently into the English epigram until the Restoration.

36. Peacham pays tribute to Ben in *Thalia's Banquet,* ep. 5 Cf. below, p. 65.

37. This element, of course, appeared in the *Greek Anthology,* 186 ff., eps. 56, 118, 442. See also Mackail, *Select Epigrams,* pp. 65–66. Peacham might have wished to change the adage to read, *Vivamus, non amemus.* In *Minerva Britanna* (1612), em. 175, he makes typical use of mythology in advising people to imitate Diana, who escaped love by hunting.

38. *The More the Merrier,* sig. C 4 verso—D 1. See above, p. 53, n. 16.

39. *Minerva Britanna* (1612), "To the Reader," sig. A 3.

40. Miss Pitman, "Studies of Peacham," p. 166, shows the relation between the set-up of Peacham's and Whitney's emblems (Geoffrey Whitney, *A Choice of Emblems,* 1586).

41. See Hakluyt's *Principal Navigations,* Glasgow, 1903–5, 12 vols., XII, p. 97.

42. Here again he parallels his fellow townsman John Heywood, who wrote:

    In all my simple writyng never ment I
    To touche any private person displeasantly.

    See Heywood, *The Proverbs and Epigrams of John Heywood,* 2 vols., Spenser Society Publications (1867), I, p. 174.

43. *The More the Merrier,* sig. A 3. Later still (ep. 43) he advises his fellow poet not to write anything "in private hate."

44. *Thalia's Banquet,* ep. 123.

45. Ibid., ep. 2.

46. *Epigrams,* ep. 23, p. 98.

47. *Thalia's Banquet,* sig. A 4.

48. There is always the problem of just what the seventeenth century meant by "wit."

49. *Thalia's Banquet,* eps. 108, 109.

Miss Pitman, "Studies of Peacham," p. 165, points out the "humourous turn of Peacham's mind" when she calls the strange language he used in the third of his verses to Coryat as "an early ancestor of Lewis Carroll's Jabberwocky." See *Coryat's Crudities,* 2 vols., Glasgow (1905) I, p. 115:

> Ny thalonin ythsi Coryate lachmah babowans
> O Asiam Europam Americ-werowans
> Poph-himgi Savoya, Hessen, Rhetia, Ragonzie
> France, Germanien dove Anda-louzie
> Not A-rag-on ô Coryate, ô hone vilascar
> Einen tronk Od-combe ny Venice Berga-mascar.

Perhaps the above might better be characterized as macaronic verse!

50. *The More the Merrier,* sig. A 4.

51. Ibid., sig. B 1.

51a. See above, pp. 39–40.

52. *Minerva Britanna* (1612) em. 101. With a poet's pride, he claims poetry outlasts all (em. 161). Cf. above, p. 40, n. 32.

53. "Studies of Peacham," p. 48.

54. *Minerva Britanna* (1612), em. 74.

55. Ibid., em. 75. Cf. above, p. 46, n. 73.

56. *Minerva Britanna* (1612), em. 109.

57. *Paradise Lost,* VIII, 167–78.

58. *Minerva Britanna* (1612), em. 178. He had voiced the same thought in em. 156. Cf. below, p. 63.

59. Ibid., em. 159.

60. Ibid., em. 192. He quotes Cicero on the occasion.

61. His interests were wide. In *The More the Merrier,* sig. A 2 verso, he confesses that his verses involve religion, politics, and the law. In ep. 43 of the same work he compares the variety of his interests to the many parts of St. Paul's. Further, he writes (ep. 43), "this head of mine with sundry humors fraught;" and he specifically mentions taking more than ordinary interest in music, painting, "guilding," business, and war. He was at times inclined to deplore his versatility. In "To the Reader" of *Truth* sig. A 5–A 5 verso, he wrote: "I have ever found multiplicity of Knowledge in many things to hav beene rather an hinderance, then ever any Way tending to advancement."

62. *Minerva Britanna* (1612), em. 184.

63. Em. 206.

64. F. W. Moorman (*Robert Herrick: A Biographical and Critical Study,* London and New York [1910], pp. 283–84) makes the point that Herrick's epigrams are

coarser than the rest of his poems because, presumably, that was what was expected of the epigram.

65. *Epigrams,* p. 22. He speaks there of "the free plainness of expression, that is, for the language of the epigram."

66. Ibid., p. 164, ep. 69.

67. Everard Guilpin, *Skialetheia,* London (1598), ep. 47.

68. Bastard, *Chrestoleros. Seven Books of Epigrames* (1598), reprint ed., Spenser Society (1888), p. 3.

69. *Flowers of Epigrammes* (1577), reprint ed., Spenser Society (1874), p. 9. In ep. 19 Kendall has:

    Martial is muche mislikt, and lothde, of modest mynded men:
    For leude lascivious wanton woorks, and woords which he doeth pen.
    ....
    His woorks are like a garden good, with weedes muche overgrowen:
    Lo reader here the fragrant flowers, the weedes awaie are throwen.

70. *The More the Merrier,* Dedicatory Epistle, sig. A 2.
His "honest tearmes" of ep. 43 (bis) amount to the same.

71. *Thalia's Banquet,* ep. 127. In *Thestylis Atrata,* he scorns the lecher who prefers the "draughts of Aretine" to the noble work of Michelangelo. Sig. C 3 verso. Aretine appears to have stood to him as the very symbol of indecency; in *The Art of Drawing,* p. 9, Peacham condemns him for "his booke and baudy pictures."

72. *The More the Merrier,* ep. 45.

73. *Thalia's Banquet,* ep. 74.

74. Ibid., ep. 124. For other examples see eps. 27, 28.

75. More was a fellow townsman.

76. *Coach and Sedan,* London (1925).

77. *The More the Merrier,* sig. A 2 verso.

78. *The Epigrams of Sir John Harington,* ed. N. E. McClure, Philadelphia (1926), p. 90.
Since the bulk of Harington's epigrams saw print after *The More the Merrier* (1608), the borrowing, if any, may have been the other way. On the other hand, most of Harington's, as Whipple says *(Martial and the English Epigram,* p. 345), were written by 1600 and, in light of the way popular manuscripts were passed around in those days, the chances are good that Peacham was the debtor, if indeed there was any case of borrowing. John Davies has "a leaden rapier in a golden sheath" (quoted by Whipple, *Martial and the English Epigram,* p. 379). Cf. above, p. 54.

79. *The More the Merrier,* sig. A 2 verso.

80. Ibid., ep. 53.

81. *Thalia's Banquet,* ep. 114.

81a. See above, p. 33.

82. *Epigrams,* p. 309, ep. 12. Martial protests further: "No portion of reputation, obtained at the expense of another, is pleasing in my eyes."

82a. See above, p. 49, n. 111.

83. *Minerva Britanna,* (1612) em. 57.

84. *Martial's Epigrams,* II, p. 29.

85. Ibid., II, 359.

86. *The More the Merrier,* ep. 51.

87. *Thalia's Banquet,* ep. 76.

88. Ibid., ep. 21.

89. *The More the Merrier,* ep. 31.

90. In *The Valley of Varietie,* p. 68, he does refer to "the Turks, Persians, and other Barbarians." But in the seventeenth century there was nothing unusual about such an allusion.

91. *Thalia's Banquet,* ep. 111.

92. Ibid., ep. 41.

93. Ibid., ep. 121.

94. Ibid., ep. 120.

95. *Minerva,* em. 208.

96. Flora, Roman goddess of blooming vegetation.

97. *Minerva Britanna* (1612), em. 175.

98. Ibid., em. 156.

> Who knowes to speake, and when to hold his peace,
> Findes fewest daungers, and lives best at ease.

99. *Thalia's Banquet,* ep. 92.

100. In *The Compleat Gentleman,* p. 51, he wrote: "No subject affecteth us with more delight then *History,* imprinting a thousand formes upon our imaginations, from the circumstances of Place, Person, Time, Matter, manner, and the like." This interest is ever-present. It is probable he knew how the Greek historians used epigrams as dependable sources of information.

The sixth vision in *The Period of Mourning* contains much history. Not satisfied with the amount conveyed in the text, he writes long prose elaborations. For the *Nuptiall Hymnes,* that follow *The Period* in the original edition, he similarly writes extended notes (many of them on Roman history as well as on heraldry and legend). In *Thestylis Atrata* the numerous notes, in which he shows much detailed knowledge, are run right in the text. *Prince Henrie Revived,* sig. B 4 verso, has quite a few lines tracing history, both European and English. *The Valley of Varietie* (p. 74) has an exact description of Roman Triumphs. See below, p. 99 and Appendix.

101. *Minerva Britanna* (1612), em. 90.

102. *Thestylis Atrata,* em. 208.

103. Sig. B 2 verso. He spends several pages, in the manner of Tom Fuller, telling of Lincolnshire's famous people. See below, p. 107 and Appendix.

104. In *Minerva Britanna* (1612), em. 29 is addressed to "Edward Coke, Lord cheife Justice."

105. *Thalia's Banquet,* ep. 116.

106. *The More the Merrier,* ep. 5. It is obvious that such stories have a close connection with the popular jest books.

107. Ibid., ep. 16.

108. Ibid., ep. 47.

109. *Thalia's Banquet,* ep. 19.

110. Ibid., ep. 119.

111. See R. R. Cawley, *Studies in Sir Thomas Browne,* Oregon University Press (1965), pp. 7–33.

112. *Minerva Britanna* (1612), em. 154.

113. Ibid., em. 152.

114. On the other hand, there is evidence that he had made considerably more than a superficial study of natural history. For instance, in emblem 208 of *Minerva Britanna* he goes into detail about various animals, especially birds.

115. *Thalia's Banquet,* ep. 38.

116. *Minerva Britanna* (1612), em. 208, p. 212.

117. *Thalia's Banquet,* ep. 5. In *Truth,* pp. 37–38, Peacham records the well known story about Spenser: "The famous *Spencer* did never get any preferment in his life, save toward his latter end hee became a Clerk of the Councell in *Ireland;* and dying in *England,* hee dyed but poore. When he lay sick, the Noble, and patterne of true Honour, *Robert,* Earle of *Essex,* sent him twenty pound, either to relieve or bury him."

118. *Thalia's Banquet,* ep. 80.

119. *The More the Merrier,* ep. 34.

120. Ibid., sig. A 3 verso.

121. See his reference to "famous Moore," above, p. 42.

122. *Minerva Britanna* (1612), em. 34.

123. Peacham quite properly addresses him as "learned Sir." It will be recalled that "I.S." (almost certainly John Selden) contributed a Greek poem and two poems in Latin to the volume in which *The Period of Mourning* appeared. See Pitman, "Studies of Peacham," pp. 170–1.

124. *The More the Merrier,* sig. A 3 verso.

125. The following has the ring of genuine appreciation in spite of its figures being in part derived:

    How oft hereof the Image I admire,
    In thee sweete *Musick,* Natures chast delight,
    The Banquets frend, and Ladie of the Quire;
    Phisition to the melancholly spright:
    Mild Nurse of Pietie, ill vices foe;
    Our Passions Queene, and Soule of All below.

    The marginal note shows technical knowledge of music *(Minerva Britanna,* em. 204).

126. *Thalia's Banquet,* ep. 97. Probably few seventeenth-century poets could have resisted the pun, *"Never such a bird"* for singing.

127. Ibid., ep. 99.

128. *Minerva Britanna* (1612), em. 74. Peacham blames the public for neglecting Dowland in his old age: "How few regard thee, whome thou didst delight."
In "Studies of Peacham," p. 164, Miss Pitman calls our attention to the fact that Peacham wrote a poem in Latin for Dowland's son Robert.

129. *Minerva Britanna* (1612), em. 101.

130. *Thalia's Banquet*, ep. 121.

131. *Minerva Britanna* (1612), em. 92.

132. Ibid., em. 89.

133. *Thalia's Banquet*, ep. 42.

134. Ibid., ep. 58.

135. Ibid., ep. 63.

136. Ibid., ep. 49.

137. Ibid., ep. 55.

138. *Thestylis Atrata*, sig. B 2 verso.

THE ELEGY

1. See F. W. Weitzmann, "Notes on the Elizabethan *Elegie*," PMLA, vol. L, 435–43, for a brief study. The elegy as a whole has not received the treatment it deserves.

2. For a pre-Elizabethan example we have Surrey's three poems on Wyatt, two of them in sonnet form. See *Henry Howard Earl of Surrey: Poems*, Oxford (1964), pp. 27–29. With his spiritual closeness to Wyatt, Surrey has succeeded in giving a personal impression of the man, stressing the envy that had grown up around his hero. Surrey's epitaph may well have been his first appearance in verse.
In the next century Henry King in *Poems*, ed. Margaret Crum, Oxford (1965), p. 66, brings his subject alive in his "Elegy Upon S[ir] W[alter] R[alegh]," by attacking his envious foes,

   Who when they thought to make thee scandall's story,
   Lent thee a swifter flight to heav'n and glory.

3. Ruth Wallerstein, *Studies in Seventeenth-Century Poetic*, Madison, Wis. (1950), p. 67 (hereafter cited as *Studies in Poetic*). Miss Wallerstein distinguishes the genre from the main stream, and especially differentiates the pastoral elegies from the Prince Henry elegies (see p. 95).

4. Various other poets contributed elegies to Spenser's volume.

5. Edward Herbert of Cherbury, *Poems*, Oxford (1923), p. 53.

6. Joshua Sylvester, *Complete Works*, 2 vols., Edinburgh, (1880), II, p. 339.

7. John Lane, *Fugitive Poetical Tracts*, 2nd series, Roxburghe Library, n.d.

8. Giles and Phineas Fletcher, *Poetical Works,* ed. Boas, 2 vols., Cambridge (1908), I, pp. 1–3. Giles was a fledgling in his 'teens when the Queen died.

9. Ibid., I, pp. 92–94.

10. John Fenton, *King James: His Welcome to London,* London (1603), sig. B 2.

11. It is printed in *Harleian Miscellany,* vol. III (1745), pp. 500–18. The work is discussed at some length in Harold Jenkins' *Life and Works of Henry Chettle,* London (1934), pp. 48–53.

12. On this tradition see *The Pastoral Elegy: An Anthology,* ed. T. P. Harrison, Jr., University of Texas, Austin (c. 1939). Miss Wallerstein *Studies in Poetic,* p. 67, gives her definition of the pastoral elegy.

13. Peacham's own commemoration is in *Prince Henrie Revived,* sig. C 2. He refers to her as

    Eliza Queene, the Maiden conqueresse,
    Borne in triumphall Charriot.

14. John W. Draper, *The Funeral Elegy and the Rise of English Romanticism,* New York University Press (1929), p. 45. Draper has also issued *A Century of Broadside Elegies,* London (1928). In this collection are ninety English elegies and ten Scottish ones. Peacham rates only one note (p. 99) in Draper's monumental volume.

15. Draper, *The Funeral Elegy,* p. 27.

16. We should, however, not forget that "Adonais," "In Memoriam," and "Thyrsis" purvey considerably more than details about the deaths of Keats, Hallam, and Clough.

17. James Holly, *A Milton Handbook,* New York (1926), p. 107.

18. *Poems,* 2 vols., London and New York (1894), II, pp. 287–97.

19. Ibid., II, p. 292.

20. Ibid., II, pp. 293–94.

21. Francis Quarles, *Complete Works in Prose and Verse,* 3 vols. (1880), III, sec. X.

22. Ibid., III, pp. 3–8.

23. See Wallerstein, *Studies in Poetic,* pp. 91–92. Miss Wallerstein confers knighthood upon him. See pp. 91, 358.

24. Richard Crashaw, *Poems,* ed. L. C. Martin, Oxford (1957), p. 167, ll. 35–40.

25. Ibid., p. 175.

26. Michael Drayton, *Works,* ed. Hebel, 5 vols., Oxford (1931–41), III (1961), pp. 242–3.

27. William Drummond, *Poems,* 2 vols., London and New York (1894), II, p. 109.

28. Ibid., II, p. 170.

29. *Studies in Poetic,* p. 97.

30. Ibid., p. 102.

31. Cleveland, *Poems of John Cleveland,* Oxford (1967), p. 1, ll. 5–6.

32. Robert Greene, *Plays and Poems of R. G.,* ed. J. C. Collins, 2 vols., Oxford (1905), II, pp. 221–35.

33. Webster, John, *Works,* ed. Alexander Dyce, London (1857), pp. 371–76. Wither says much the same in his poem on Henry, claiming he "Doth neither write for Praise, nor hope of Gaine." See George Wither, *Poems. Juvenilia.* Printed for the Spenser Society (1871), pp. 369–87.

34. *An Aprill Shower,* p. 2.

35. Cyril Tourneur, *Works,* ed. Allardyce Nicoll, London (1929), p. 155. Waller wrote (pp. 22–23) "The Countess of Carlisle in Mourning" as well as "To My Lord Northumberland Upon the Death of his Lady" (pp. 31–32).

36. Drummond, *Poems,* II, pp. 113–117.

37. Brooke, *Complete Poems,* ed. Grosart, Fuller's Worthies (1872), pp. 203–21.

38. Edmund Waller, *Poems,* ed. G. Thorn Drury, London and New York (1893), pp. 37–40. Bishop Henry King wrote on the same lady in his *Poems,* pp. 93–95.

39. Ben Jonson, *Poems,* ed. Newdigate, Oxford (1936), pp. 199–202 and pp. 202–8.

40. Drayton wrote also on Sir Henry Raynsford and "Upon the three Sonnes of Lord Sheffield, Drowned in Humber."

41. Thomas Carew, *Poems,* Oxford (1949), pp. 67, 69.

42. Wither, *Poems . Juvenilia,* p. 369.

43. John Taylor, *Works.* Printed for Spenser Society (1869), p. 468 ff. Taylor has a whole series of elegies addressed to dukes, earls, and others of high birth.

44. *Thestylis Atrata,* sig. A 3.

45. Ibid., sig. A 2.

46. Richard James, *Poems,* ed. Grosart, printed for Private Circulation (1880), pp. 106–31.

47. Taylor, *Works,* pp. 322–26.

48. Chettle, *Poems,* p. 24.

49. See *Harleian Miscellany,* vol. III (1745), pp. 517–18. Chettle's poem is in the pastoral elegy tradition.

50. Giles and Phineas Fletcher, *Poetical Works,* I, pp. 92–94. Once more, classical and pastoral imagery get in the way of any feeling.

51. One gets the impression that elegists were hard put to find things to praise.

52. Campion, *Works,* ed. P. Vivian, Oxford (1906; reprinted ed. 1966), pp. 106–7.

53. George Chapman, *Poems,* ed. P. B. Bartlett, Oxford (1941), pp. 251–68.

54. *Prince Henrie Revived,* sig. D 1:

> Thy Grandsire *James,* our Royall *Mercurie:*
> Who with his wand all tumult caus'd to cease,
> Fulfill'd our wishes, gave our daies their peace.

55. See E. C. Wilson, *Prince Henry and English Literature,* Ithaca (1946), pp. 151, 169 (hereafter cited as *Prince Henry).*

56. Hannay, *Poetical Works,* London, (1622), pp. 185–92 and 195–204. The level of poetry may be judged from the following:

> Let them straine inward, if they'le needs distill,
> And with their drops thy *hearts* sad *center* fill,
> And when *it's* full, *it* can no more containe,
> Let the *caske* breake, and drowne *thee* in that *maine.*

57. Campion, *Works,* pp. 106–7.

58. Wither, *Poems. Juvenilia,* pp. 353–99.

59. "To the Queene's Maiestye," Gorges, *The Olympian Catastrophe,* Kensington (1925).

60. Donne, *Poems,* ed. H. J. C. Grierson, 2 vols., Oxford (1912), I, pp. 371–95.

61. Ibid., II, p. 254 ff.

62. *Poems English and Latin of Edward Lord Herbert of Cherbury,* ed. Moore Smith, Oxford (1923), pp. 57–59, 11.61–62.

63. His "Elegie" is included by Grierson in *Poems,* I, pp. 376–77, 11.2–3.

64. His contribution is printed by Grierson in *Poems,* I, pp. 386–88. There is some question whether the poem is Brathwaite's. Grierson (II, p. 259), following Gosse, says he "is perhaps the most likely candidate for the initials."

65. Grierson prints the elegy, ibid., I, pp. 371–72.

66. It is to be hoped that Miss Crum's handsome recent edition may help to reestablish King's poetic importance. See *Poems of Henry King,* ed. Margaret Crum, Oxford, (1965).

67. King, *Poems,* pp. 87–88.

68. Scholars dispute over whether "To the Memory of Ben Jonson" is Cleveland's or not. In his edition of Cleveland's *Poems,* Berdan prints it under "Poems Attributed to Cleveland by Modern Scholars"; but it is not included by Morris and Withington in their edition of his *Poems,* Oxford (1967), and they say (p. 176), "this piece is surely not by Cleveland." At any rate, the poem is of little consequence. Preceding the above poem is "An Elegy on Ben Jonson," which Berdan thinks to be definitely Cleveland's; but once more the Oxford editors fail to include it.

69. Wallerstein, *Studies in Poetic,* pp. 96–114. In her Appendix she prints Beaumont's poem (pp. 361–65) and More's (pp. 365–66).

70. Ibid., p. 103.

71. Thomas Birch, Secretary of the Royal Society, was Henry's formal biographer. See *The Life of Henry Prince of Wales, Eldest Son of King James I,* London (1760). See also Sir Charles Cornwallis, *The Life and Death of Our Late Most Incomparable and Heroique Prince, Henry Prince of Wales,* London (1641), as well as James Maxwell's *The Laudable Life and Deplorable Death of Our Late Peerlesse Prince Henry,* (London), 1612.

    E. C. Wilson *(Prince Henry,* p. 132 n.) notes that John Philip Edmond "about 1901" compiled a bibliography of the elegies which were printed 1612–14. See *Publications of the Edinburgh Bibliographical Society,* VI (1906), 141–58.

72. E. C. Wilson *(Prince Henry,* p. 153) argues with conviction that Milton knew Drummond's *Teares on . . . Moeliades* [Prince Henry], and possibly Sylvester's *Lachrymae Lachrymarum* (see pp. 154–55).

73. Wilson, *Prince Henry,* p. 151.

    Miss Wallerstein analyzes quite a few of the elegies in her third chapter. See *Studies in Poetic,* pp. 59–95. Her approach is consistently philosophic and aesthetic. At the beginning of her fourth chapter (p. 96) she lists what she considers the dominating influences on the Henry elegies.

74. His early death, at eighteen, naturally added to the myth. Wither gives the best poetic description of the physical circumstances of the funeral in *Poems. Juvenilia,* elegy 34. "Blacke was White-hall . . . Hung all with sacke, or sable-cloth of haire."

75. Bacon's is a characteristically restrained estimate: "Many points there were indeed in this prince's nature which were obscure, and could not be discovered by any man's judgment, but only by time, which was not allowed him. Those however which appeared were excellent; which is enough for fame." *Works,* VI, p. 329.

76. Sig. A 2 verso. Quoted by E. C. Wilson, *Prince Henry,* p. 82.

77. Ibid., p. 145, n. 45.

78. Ibid., pp. 142–44.

79. *The Masque of Queens* was also intended to honor the prince. See Wilson, *Prince Henry,* pp. 70–71.

80. See Bacon, *Works,* XI (1868), pp. 340–341.

81. Ibid., VI, p. 328.

82. Wilson, *Prince Henry,* p. 173. For other works dedicated to Henry see pp. 90–93 and 103–16.

83. Ibid., p. 149.

84. But he goes on to say that the many elegies "helped keep supple the English genius for the form" (p. 150).

85. Wallerstein, *Studies in Poetic,* p. 96. In her Appendix she conveniently reproduces many of the poems, some of them hard to find in libraries.

86. See Wilson, *Prince Henry,* p. 157.

87. John Taylor, in "Great Britaine, all in blacke," summarizes them all in a single line when he speaks of Henry leading "The life of Peace, of War, of Court, of Campe."

88. See Wilson, *Prince Henry,* p. 94.

89. Ibid., p. 114.

90. Drummond, *Poems,* 2 vols., London and New York, 1894, II, p. 7, 11. 61–2.

91. Taylor, *Works* (1869), p. 474.

92. Wilson, *Prince Henry,* p. 137. Brooke instead chose Mars' mate: "Bellona was his goddesse." See Christopher Brooke, *Complete Poems,* ed. Grossart (1872), p. 183.

93. Webster actually draws the comparison with the Black Prince. See his *Monumental Columne* in *Complete Works,* ed. F. L. Lucas, 4 vols., London (1927), vol. III, p. 276.

94. John Davies of Hereford, *Muses-teares,* London (1613), sig. A 2. Similarly Robert Allyne stresses Henry's prowess. See *Funerall Elegies,* (1613), sigs. A 3 verso–A 4.

95. Campion, *Works,* p. 104.

96. James Maxwell, "The Memorable Life and Death of Our Late Peerelesse Prince Henry," stanza 25, in *Laudable Life.*

97. Wilson, *Prince Henry,* p. 135.

98. Gorges, *The Olympian Catastrophe.*

99. Wilson, *Prince Henry,* p. 137.

100. In acknowledging gifts from a Frenchman, Henry wrote: "You have sent me a present of the two things which I most delight in, arms and horses." See Wilson, *Prince Henry,* p. 62.

101. Maxwell, "Memorable Life," st. 25 in *Laudable Life.*

102. Webster, *Monumental Columne, Complete Works,* (1927), III, p. 276. Brooke in *Complete Poems,* p. 181, wrote:

> that Mars with wit's Minerva seem'd at jarre,
> Which of them both should sway his princely hart.

103. Brooke, *Complete Poems,* p. 181.

104. Thomas Heywood, *A Funerall Elegie,* London (1613), sig. B 3 verso.

105. Gorges, *The Olympian Catastrophe,* p. 23.

106. Quoted by Wilson, *Prince Henry,* p. 141.

107. *The Period of Mourning,* London (1789), p. 22. Actually, the lines occur in "An Elegiack Epitaph," which follows *The Period.*

108. Maxwell, "Memorable Life," ep. 1, in *Laudable Life.*

109. Cyril Tourneur says Henry's loss is shown, "In ev'rie *Souldiers* griefe, and *Schollars* teares." Quoted by Wilson, *Prince Henry,* p. 139.

109a. Cf. above, pp. 76–78.

110. *Minerva Britanna* (1612), sig. A 2.

111. Quoted by Wilson, *Prince Henry,* p. 114.

112. Ms. Royal.16.E.xxxviii.

113. Pitman, "Studies of Peacham," p. 282.

114. Maxwell, "Memorable Life," st. 23, *Laudable Life.*

115. Webster, *Monumental Columne,* quoted by Wilson, *Prince Henry,* p. 144.

116. Wither, *Poems. Juvenilia,* elegies 35 and 36.

117. Quoted by Wilson, *Prince Henry,* p. 145.

118. Gorges, *The Olympian Catastrophe,* p. 48.

119. *The Period* (1789), p. 5.

120. *The Period of Mourning,* London (1613), p. 17.

121. *The Period* (1789), p. 22.

122. Tourneur stresses that Henry was a patron of learning (see "A Griefe on the Death of Prince Henrie" in *Works,* London [1929] pp. 265–70); and this side of his character is a constant theme in the Oxford and Cambridge elegies.

123. Quoted by Wilson, *Prince Henry,* p. 139. There has even been some talk about the prince's books having contributed importantly to the British Museum. See Wilson, *Prince Henry,* pp. 171–72.

124. Quoted in Wilson, *Prince Henry,* p. 139. Wither shows something of the same courage when he advises Charles to imitate Henry's virtues. See *Poems. Juvenilia,* p. 402.

125. *The Period* (1613), sig. D 2.

126. Heywood, *A Funerall Elegie,* sig. B 3 verso.

127. Sylvester has in mind the same combination when he insists that all who love *"Religion, Armes, or Art"* mourn the loss of Henry. *Lachrymae Lachrymarum.* Quoted by Wilson, *Prince Henry,* p. 134. Maxwell also lays great emphasis on Henry's religiosity in *Laudable Life.*

128. In the University Collections Henry is often referred to as a bulwark against the papists.

129. Quoted by Wilson, *Prince Henry,* p. 134.

130. Ibid., p. 137.

131. Wither, *Poems. Juvenilia,* p. 402.

132. Quoted by Wilson, *Prince Henry,* p. 137.

133. Ibid., p. 138.

134. Wither, *Prince Henries Obsequies* in *Poems. Juvenilia,* elegy 35.

135. Ibid., elegy 37.

136. See Wilson, *Prince Henry,* p. 137.

137. Campion, *Works,* pp. 104–5. In his *Epicede,* Chapman resorts to a comparison with Gates' famous wreck on the Bermudas, of which Shakespeare made good use in *The Tempest.* See George Chapman, *Poems of George Chapman,* ed. P. B. Bartlett, Oxford (1941), pp. 251–68, 1. 491 ff.

138. Quoted by Wilson, *Prince Henry,* p. 136. Similarly Wither says, "the turkie *Moone* look't pale." Ibid., p. 137.

139. Wither, *Obsequies, Poems. Juvenilia,* elegy 27.

140. Quoted by Wilson, *Prince Henry,* p. 143.

141. Henry King, *Poems,* p. 65. See bib.

142. Gorges, *The Olympian Catastrophe,* p. 57.

143. Goodyere and Heywood make exactly the same point. See Wallerstein, *Studies in Poetic,* p. 82 and Heywood's *Funerall Elegie,* 1613, st. 3.

144. Taylor, *Works* (1869), p. 474.

145. John Webster, *Works,* ed. Alexander Dyce, London (1857), p. 375.

146. Wither, *Obsequies, Poems. Juvenilia,* elegies 19, 22.

147. Thomas Heywood, *A Marriage Triumph,* London (1842), p. 3.

148. Thomas Heywood, *A Funerall Elegie,* sig. A 3.

149. Similarly Campion *(Works,* p. 104), Chapman *(Poems,* pp. 251–68, "An Epicede"), and Herbert of Cherbury *(Poems,* pp. 22–24), all berate Death (or Fate) in vigorous language.

Drummond wrote on Sir Anthony Alexander:

> O Death! what treasure in one hour
> Hast thou dispersed! how dost thou devour
> What we on earth hold dearest!

See Drummond, *Poems,* II, p. 113, 11. 15–17.

150. William Basse, *Poetical Works,* ed. R. W. Bond, London (1893) p. 95.

151. Michael Drayton, *Poems,* ed. John Buxton, 2 vols., London (1953), I, pp. 160–62, ll. 57–58.

152. Brooke, *Complete Poems,* p. 185.

153. Donne, *Poems,* I, p. 281, l. 60.

154. Crashaw, *Poems,* p. 172, ll. 9–12. Cf. Drummond, *Poems,* II, p. 176, ll. 9–10.

155. William Basse, *Great Brittaines Sunnes-set,* Oxford (1613), stanza 16.

156. Sylvester, *Lacrymae Lacrymarum,* l. 138 ff, in *Complete Works,* II, pp. 275–78.

157. Ibid., ll. 113–14.

For, for the *People's* Sins for *Subjects'* Crimes,
God takes-away good *Princes* oftentimes.

158. Wither, *Poems. Juvenilia,* elegy 41.

159. Heywood, *A Funerall Elegie,* sig. B 3.

160. Heywood, *A Marriage Triumph,* p. 3.

161. Sylvester, *Lacrymae Lacrymarum, Complete Works,* II, pp. 275–78.

162. William Alexander, *Poetical Works,* ed. L. E. Kastner, 2 vols., Edinburgh and London (1921–29), II, pp. 527–30.

163. Drummond, *Poems,* II, p. 113, l. 18.

164. Brooke, *Complete Poems,* p. 188.

165. Gorges, *Olympian Catastrophe,* p. 48.

166. Chapman, *Poems,* p. 251, ll. 15–17.

167. Sylvester, *Complete Works,* II, pp. 275–78, l. 138.

168. Heywood, *A Funerall Elegie,* sig. C 1 verso: "Death is to *Him* a Gain."

169. Basse, *Great Brittaines Sunnes-set,* stanza 8.

170. Giles and Phineas Fletcher, *Poetical Works,* I, p. 268.

171. Cited by Wilson, *Prince Henry,* p. 163.

172. Quoted by Wilson, *Prince Henry,* p. 94.

173. Webster, *A Monumental Columne* in *Complete Works* (1927), III, pp. 275–83.

174. Gorges, *The Olympian Catastrophe,* pp. 51, 53.

175. Drummond, *Poems,* I, p. 11, ll. 173–75.

176. *The Period* (1789), p. 23.

177. Browne, *An Elegy,* London (1613).

178. Gorges, *The Olympian Catastrophe,* p. 23.

179. Henry King, *Poems,* p. 65, ll. 15–16.

180. Wither, "Prince Henries Obsequies," *Poems. Juvenilia,* elegy 41.

181. T. Heywood, *Funerall Elegie,* sig. A 3, stanza 3.

In his elegy Donne says that Henry's death amounts to the death of all England.

182. Giles and Phineas Fletcher, *Poetical Works,* I, p. 266.

183. Browne, *Poems,* I, p. 276, stanza 8:

Britain was whilom known, by more than fame,
To be one of the islands fortunate.

184. Sylvester, *Lacrymae Lacrymarum,* ll. 59–60, *Complete Works,* II.

185. Gorges, *The Olympian Catastrophe,* p. 50.

186. It is Mercury chosen also in *Chesters triumph* to speak for all the gods about "thy vertues generall" (quoted by Wilson, *Prince Henry,* p. 82). Maxwell maintains there is no virtue Henry does not possess (p. 133). And in the masque *Oberon* the Prince is referred to as "the height of all our race" (p. 93). Basse uses the same figure, "like a high Pyramis." See *Poetical Works,* pp. 87–100, stanza 14. The *reductio* is reached in Wither's declaring in "Prince Henries Obsequies," elegy 21, that when Henry was emboweled, no gall was found in him, "he was sweetnesse all"! The fact that this story was a matter of some common knowledge is shown by Davies of Hereford's alluding to it in *Complete Works,* I, p. 5 and n. 1.

187. Alexander, *An Elegie, Poetical Works,* II, pp. 527–30, l. 98.

188. Giles and Phineas Fletcher, *Poetical Works,* I, p. 268.

189. John Davies of Hereford, *Complete Works,* ed. Grossart, 2 vols. (1878), I, p. 6.

190. Other examples of hyperbole follow:

> Hath not her wat'ry zone, in murmuring,
> Fill'd every shore with echoes of her cry?
> Yes, Thetis raves,
> And bids her waves
> Bring all the nymphs within her Empery
> To be assistant in her sorrowing.
> See where they sadly sit on Isis' shore,
> And rend their hairs as they would joy no more.
> (William Browne, *Poems,* I, p. 276.)

The above is perhaps the best instance of extreme use of the pathetic fallacy.

> Well could I wish, (but wishing is in vaine)
> That many millions, and amongst them I
> Had sluc'd the bloods from every flowing veine,
> And vented floods of water from each eye.
> (Taylor, *Works* (1869), p. 474.)

> As if your teares (like floods that overflowe
> Their liquid shores) alone would have excell'd
> This generall *Deluge* of our eies, that so
> Sea-like our earth-like cheekes hath over-swell'd.
> (Basse, *Great Brittaines Sunnes-set,* stanza 3.)

As if to make up, in part, Basse has in the next stanza a line, with effective use of alliteration, that is worthy of Shakespeare himself: "He loves the living best who for the dead mournes most."

191. Wallerstein, *Studies in Poetic,* p. 68.

192. Ibid., pp. 357–58.

193. Reprinted in part in Wallerstein, *Studies in Poetic,* pp. 365–66.

194. Herbert of Cherbury, *Poems,* pp. 57–59.

195. James Maxwell, *A Monument of Remembrance,* London(1613), p. 163.
Maxwell thinks of Henry's spirit guiding her ship when she sails for Germany on a voyage which Henry himself had hoped to take with her. See Wilson, *Prince Henry,* pp. 162–63.

196. Basse, *Poetical Works,* pp. 99–100.

197. Quoted by Wilson, *Prince Henry,* pp. 161–62.

198. Wither, *Poems. Juvenilia,* p. 353.

199. T. Heywood, *A Funerall Elegie,* sig. C 1 verso.

200. T. Heywood, *A Marriage Triumph,* p. 3.

201. See Campion, *Works,* p. 108.

202. Quoted by Wilson, *Prince Henry,* pp. 166–67.

203. *The Period,* sig. A 3 verso.

204. *Prince Henrie Revived,* sig. A 2. In *The Manner of the Solemnization of this Royall Marriage* in *The Period* (1613), sig. H 2, Peacham goes into great detail about the wedding. In the 1789 edition of *The Period* the passage appears on pp. 50–51.

205. Quoted by Wilson, *Prince Henry,* pp. 161–62.

206. *Poetical Works* (1893), p. 100.

207. Quoted by Wilson, *Prince Henry,* p. 167.

208. In "To the Muse," *The Period* (1613), sig. A 3 verso, he writes "since thou hast beene asleep."

209. *Prince Henrie Revived,* sig. C 1 verso. Alas, fates were even crueler to him, dying at an earlier age than his princely uncle; his ship capsized in Haarlem Mere!

210. *The Period* (1613), sig. G 3.

211. Quoted by Wilson, *Prince Henry,* p. 163.

212. At the end of *The Laudable Life . . . of Prince Henry.*

213. Wither, "Obsequies," *Poems, Juvenilia,* p. 380, elegy 7.

214. *An Aprill Shower* (1624), p. 4. At the end of *The Period of Mourning* Peacham spoke of

That lovely cheere and gracefull Majestie
In hopefull *Charles.*

PEACHAM AND THE ELEGY

1. *The Period* (1789), p. 4.

2. Ibid., pp. 17–21.

3. Ibid., p. 21.

4. Ibid., pp. 22–23. In his dedication (p. 3) he implies that the lines were written "some while since."

5. Ibid., p. 21.

6. Wallerstein, *Studies in Poetic,* p. 62. The eighteenth-century editor of *The Period* says at the end (p. 45) that "There are so many beauties interpersed throughout these poems, that I cannot but wonder they have been so little known and noticed."

7. Wallerstein, *Studies in Poetic,* p. 379.

8. *Prince Henrie Revived,* sig. A 2.

9. At the same time we should not forget that the vision has some analogy with the emblem, in which Peacham was naturally interested. Whatever tended to combine poetry and the graphic arts appealed to him.

10. In the version in Van der Noot's *Theatre* "these same six visions" are specifically named. See Spenser's *Complete Poetical Works,* ed. R. E. N. Dodge, Cambridge, Mass. (1908), p. 765.

11. *The Period* (1789), p. 7.

12. Spenser, *Faerie Queene,* I, ix, 33–36.

13. Ibid., I, i, 14, 4–6.

14. *The Period* (1789). The eighteenth-century editor (p. 7) says of this vision, "This is much in Spenser's manner."

    That same editor, commenting (p. 42) on some lines in the fourth Nuptial Hymn, calls attention to "the enumeration of Sea-Nymphs in *The Faerie Queene,* Bk. 4 C. 11 S. 48. Seq." The first stanza of Peacham's Vision III has points of comparison with "Visions of Petrarch," IV.

15. Spenser, *Faerie Queene,* I, iv, 17 ff.

16. Pitman, "Studies of Peacham," p. 172.

    The pathetic fallacy contained in the lines beginning, "Come Woods . . . and Waters lend your sound, And help us to bemone our *Dions* death," stands in an interesting way between the comparable passage in Spenser's *Shepheardes Calender* (November) and *Lycidas.*

17. *The Period* (1789), p. 5.

18. Spenser, *Poetical Works,* p. 128, stanza 2.

19. Ibid., pp. 127–28, stanza 13. Cf. "But suddenly arose a tempest" with Peacham's "But sodainely the Day was overcast, A tempest" in *The Period,* stanza 4.

20. Spenser, *Poetical Works,* p. 124, stanza 9. Peacham has "a goodly Arke" and Spenser "a goodly ship."

21. *The Period* (1789), p. 6.

22. Spenser, *Poetical Works,* pp. 128–29, stanza 3. The second vision in *An Aprill Shower* (p. 7) has a laurel tree that is felled. Both passages concern poetry.

23. Spenser, *Poetical Works,* p. 124, stanza 7.

24. Ibid., p. 114, stanza 28.

25. *The Period* (1789), p. 13.

26. Ibid., pp. 22–23.

27. Spenser, *Poetical Works,* p. 129, stanza 7. In Spenser's *Faerie Queene,* I, ix, 38, Despair says man should die "that loatheth living breath."

28. Some significance may be read into the fact that Spenser added these lines to his version as published in a *Theatre for Worldlings.* Life had dealt severely with the poet in the twenty-two years between 1569 and 1591.

29. Spenser, *Poetical Works,* p. 125, stanza 3.

30. *The Period,* p. 13.

31. Spenser, *Poetical Works,* p. 125, stanza 2.

32. All of these details are within the single stanza.

33. Rosemary Freeman in *English Emblem Books,* London (1948), has shown that Peacham's emblematic literature owes something to Spenser. On p. 80 she says that he drew on Spenser in directions given in *The Gentleman's Exercise* as well as in the actual designs in his emblem books. Peacham may well have considered Spenser a source for "personified figures for masques and decorative works of all kinds." In his directions for expressing the months in *The Gentleman's Exercise,* p. 135, he tells the painter to show August "as our Spenser describeth him" (*Faerie Queene,* VII, vii, 37). Moreover, Fear is to be given as "he is described by our excellent Spenser [to ride] in Armour, at the clashing where of he looks deadly pale as afeared of himself" *The Gentleman's Exercise,* p. 27, and *Faerie Queene,* III, xiii, 12). When he comes to Dissimulation, Peacham notes that "the poet *Spenser* described her looking through a lattice." Miss Freeman says on p. 81 of *English Emblem Books* that he may have in mind one of the pairs in the Masque of Cupid *(The Gentleman's Exercise,* p. 114, and *Faerie Queene,* III, xii, 14). Miss Freeman also finds resemblances to Spenser in the colored *Basilicon Doron.* One of the emblems in *Minerva Britanna* has Pallas caught in a net by Avarice and Dissimulation; here too, Peacham may have drawn on Spenser. Miss Freeman further points out on p. 82 of *English Emblem Books* that Philautia "might well be a picture of Lucifera," and that Gula is like Spenser's figure, having the same "long neck and vast paunch."

34. See Wilson, *Prince Henry,* pp. 22–23.

35. As quoted by Wilson in *Prince Henry.*

36. Quoted by Wilson, *Prince Henry,* p. 63. Wilson also says on p. 88 that when his own ship was being built, Henry asked Ralegh for advice. Ralegh replied in a letter that still survives. It is also of interest that the great mathematician Edward Wright dedicated his new edition of *Certaine Errors in Navigation* (1610) to the prince.

37. *The Period* (1789), p. 5.

38. In "Bellay" Spenser has, "This ship, to which none other might compare." See his *Poetical Works,* p. 127, stanza 13.

39. See Wilson, *Prince Henry,* pp. 87–90.

40. Ibid., p. 63.

41. Ibid., pp. 117–18.

42. Ibid., pp. 118–19.

43. Ibid., p. 48.

44. Quoted by Wilson, *Prince Henry,* p. 119, from a narrative of 1615.

44a. Cf. above, pp. 76–80.

45. *The Period,* (1789), p. 21.

46. Ibid., p. 6.

47. Ibid., p. 13.

47a. Cf. above, p. 84.

48. *The Period* (1789), p. 8. One cannot help wondering whether Peacham had any individual in mind for the malefactor who was responsible for more deaths than Death himself!

49. Ibid., pp. 8–9.

49a. For Henry's interest in horsemanship, see above, p. 80.

50. *Period,* p. 12.

51. *The Compleat Gentleman,* ed. G. S. Gorden, Oxford (1906), p. 156 ff. Heraldry reappears prominently in "Nuptiall Hymnes," *The Period* (1789), p. 39.

51a. Cf. above, p. 87.

52. *The Period,* pp. 10–12.

53. Ibid., stanza 2:

Come every Plant that growes upon the ground,
Your fruit or savours to his Herse bequeath.

54. The "Menalcas" of the fifth stanza is introduced by Spenser in *The Shepheards Calander* (June, 1) 102.

55. Cf. above, p. 87.

55a. *The Period* (1789), p. 11.

56. Ibid., pp. 13–16.

56a. See above, p. 63.

57. It is not always possible to determine which are his notes. Even those which may be by the original editor may have been "fed" to him by Peacham. In the 1613 edition of *The Period* the notes are in the margin; the editor of 1789 reduced them to the foot of the page. These elaborate notes appear also in the *Nuptiall Hymnes* and in *Prince Henrie Revived.* In *Thestylis Atrata* they are put right in the text itself.

58. *The Period* (1789), pp. 17–21.

59. Ibid., pp. 22–23.

60. Pitman, "Studies of Peacham," p. 173.

61. This is an attitude he shared with his contemporary, Donne.
Cf. Drummond's *Teares on the Death of Moeliades,* ll. 173–74; in Heaven Henry finds,

Courts void of flattery, of malice minds,
Pleasure which lasts, not such as reason blinds.

62. Miss Pitman ("Studies of Peacham," pp. 173–4) calls our attention to Peacham's change of measure when he turned to the epithalamium in the "Nuptiall Hymnes in Honour of the Marriage between Frederick Count Palatine and Elizabeth onely Daughter to our Soveraigne" *(The Period* (1789), pp. 31–45); she speaks of how the verses "trip along to a merry rhythm." Their trippingness may be seen in such lines as the following in *The Period,* p. 33:

Nymphes of *Niger* offer Plumes:
Some your Odors and Perfumes.
Dians Maids more white then milke,
Fit a Roabe of finest Silke.

Actually, all four hymns are written in different measures. At the very beginning Peacham makes the connection with the "Visions" in *The Period* (1789), p. 31.

All Feares are fled, and from our Sphaere
The late Eclipse is vanish'd quite.

The hymns contain more pathetic fallacy, and they further show Peacham's deep interest in history, including Roman. The learned notes begin in the third hymn. His tribute to the princess is shown in *The Period* (1789), p. 44, where Venus herself comes to the wedding to adorn the bride:

About her Ivory necke shee hung
The *Nereids* tokens, which she brought along;
And with a needle curl'd her lovely haire,
Then Gallant Pearles bestow'd at either eare:
And ore her head she threw her Sindon vaile,
That farre adowne (upborne by Nimphes) did traile.

Venus (Peacham) takes her farewell of the royal pair on p. 45 of *The Period* (1789) with the fond wish:

And let me live to see betweene you twaine,
A *Caesar* borne as great as *Charlemaine*.

63. Collier, *A Bibliographical and Critical Account of the Rarest Books in the English Language,* New York (1866), p. 166.

64. *Prince Henrie Revived,* sig. A2.

65. Quoted by Collier, *The Rarest Books,* p. 167.

66. Ibid., p. 167.

67. *Prince Henrie Revived,* sig. B 1 verso.

68. Ibid., sig. B 2.

69. Ibid., sig. C 3 verso.

70. Ibid., sig. C 4 verso.

71. Ibid., sig. C 2.

72. Ibid., sig. D 1.

73. Ibid., sig. D 1 verso.

74. Ibid., sig. D 2.

75. Ibid., sig. B 3 verso.

76. Quoted by Pitman, "Studies of Peacham," p. 176. It is more in Spenser's manner than in Milton's.

77. Collier *(The Rarest Books,* p. 168) was impressed with the mingling of styles in the following passage:

But as ore Haemus, when the morne hath drawne
Her purple Curtaines, after early dawne,
To lay to view the goodly golden pawne,
Her new borne sonne y'wrapt in Rosie lawne;
Who now, aweary of his watrie bed,
Off shakes the dew from his bright burnish'd head,
And with Ambrosian smile, and gentle cheare,
Revives the world that wanted him whileare,
So us, thine owne, thou gladdest with thy birth.

78. Henry King in *Poems* (1965), pp. 67–68, writes "An Epitaph" on the same gentleman.

79. Collier (*The Rarest Books,* p. 169), on what authority I do not know, says Peacham was at the time a retainer in Dorset's household. Collier says also that the elegy is one of the scarcest of Peacham's works, "as we never saw more than one copy of it."

80. The lines are written as if to be inscribed on Dorset's tomb.

81. *An Aprill Shower,* sig. A 3–A 3 verso.

82. Ibid., p. 5.

83. Ibid., p. 6.

84. Ibid., p. 4.

85. Ibid., p. 8.

86. Collier, *The Rarest Books,* p. 171.

87. Donne, *Poems,* I, p. 279. In dedicating to Henry Jones his elegy on Prince Henry, Chapman says that his spirits have been "so stricken . . . to the earth" that the rest of his life will be condemned "to obscuritie." See Wilson, *Prince Henry,* p. 145.

88. *An Aprill Shower,* p. 4. "Rare Poet sure was *Dorset.*"

89. King, *Poems* (1965), pp. 67–68.

90. *An Aprill Shower,* sig. A 3 verso.

91. He takes care in *An Aprill Shower,* p. 2 margin, to call the countess' attention to the fact that he had two years earlier recorded her husband's notable pedigree in *The Compleat Gentleman.* See *The Compleat Gentleman,* ed. G. S. Gordon, Oxford (1906), in the section on "The Practice of Blazonry," pp. 185–8. Pedigrees were obviously one of his real interests.

92. *An Aprill Shower,* p. 2.

93. Ibid., p. 4.

94. Ibid., p. 2.

95. Ibid., p. 3.

96. Ibid., p. 5.

97. Ibid., p. 3.

98. Ibid., p. 3.

99. Ibid., p. 6.

100. Ibid., p. 7.

101. Following this second vision comes "To the Deceased Lord," in which Peacham pays a fine compliment to the earl. He says that the loves of all "concenter in thy Shrine," and he uses the comparison with Henry the Seventh's tomb at Westminster: "So was the Plot devised, that from the Center of every window a direct line came to the K ['s] hart, lying in his Grave." [Marginal note.] Peacham must have felt that the analogy was an effective one because he had already used it in *The Period of Mourning* (p. 21) with some interesting differences of phraseology.

102. In his "Epistle to the Reader," *Thestylis Atrata,* sig. A 3 verso, he protests that, "I have in a manner altogether out of my knowledge, collected the substance of what I have written; imitating those Painters, who when they cannot get the life, are faine, for the grosser lights and shadows, to be beholding to their memories."

103. Miss Pitman in "Studies of Peacham," p. 186, notes an improvement over *An Aprill Shower* in his handling of the decasyllabic couplet.

104. "Epistle," *Thestylis Atrata,* sig. A 3.

105. Ibid., sig. A 2.

106. Ibid., sig. A 2 and A 2 verso.

107. Ibid., sig. B 1.

108. These are treated at some length in the Appendix, below.

109. This mention of the countess' father provided a natural transition back to the subject of the elegy herself.

110. *Thestylis Atrata,* sig. B 4.

111. Ibid., sig. B 4 verso.

112. She was connected by marriage with Sidney's Penelope Devereux. See *Thestylis Atrata,* B 4.

113. *Thestylis Atrata,* sig. B 4 verso.

114. Ibid., sig. C 1. Four years later he was to express his contempt for these hangers-on in *The Truth of Our Times.* See the 1942 edition, p. 59 ff.

115. *Thestylis Atrata,* sig. C 1 verso.

116. *Thestylis Atrata,* sig. C 1.

117. Ibid., sig. C 2.

118. Ibid., sig. C 3–C 3 verso.

119. Ibid., sig. C 2–C 2 verso.

120. These lines remind us of Donne and Sir Thomas Browne.

121. *Thestylis Atrata,* sig. C 3.

122. Ibid., sig. C 3 verso.

123. Ibid., sig. D 1.

124. The margin indicates there is some following of Virgil here.

125. What she is made to say on the occasion is more an expression of Peacham's own *Weltschmerz:*

> "Thou trustlesse Earth, who with thy shewes untrue,
> Thy silly children dost as Babes beguile,
> Who when (poore things) have played with awhile
> Thy gauds and toyes, thou dost their cradles fit,
> And mak'st them ready for the loathed pit."
>
> (*Thestylis Atrata,* sig. D 1)

BIBLIOGRAPHY

Alexander, William. *Poetical Works.* Ed. L. E. Kastner. 2 vols. Edinburgh and London, 1921–29.

Allyne, Robert. *Funerall Elegies.* London, 1613.

Amos, Andrew. *Martial and the Moderns.* Cambridge, England, 1858.

Basse, William. *Great Brittaines Sunnes-set.* Oxford, 1613.

_________. *Poetical Works.* Ed. R. W. Bond. London, 1893.

Bastard, Thomas. *Chrestoleros. Seven Bookes of Epigrams.* London, 1598. Reprint ed., Spenser Society, 1888.

Birch, Thomas. *The Life of Henry Prince of Wales, Eldest Son of King James I.* London, 1760.

British Martial: Or an Anthology of English Epigrams, The. 2 vols. London, 1806.

Brooke, Christopher. *Complete Poems.* Ed. Grosart, Fuller's Worthies, 1872.

Browne, William. *An Elegie on . . . Henry, Prince of Wales.* London, 1613.

_________. *Poems.* 2 vols. London and New York, 1894.

Campion, Thomas. *Works.* Ed. P. Vivian. Oxford, 1906. Reprinted ed., 1966.

Carew, Thomas. *Poems.* Oxford, 1949.

Cawley, R. R. "The History and Nature of the Early Epigram." *Journal of Historical Studies,* Autumn 1968, pp. 311–25.

_________. "Sir Thomas Browne and his Reading," *PMLA,* XLVIII, 426–70.

Chapman, George. *Poems.* Ed. P. B. Bartlett. Oxford, 1941.

Chettle, Henry. *Englands Mourning Garment.* Printed in *Harleian Miscellany,* vol. III, 1745, pp. 500–18.

_________. *Life and Works.* London, 1934. See Jenkins, Harold.

Cleveland, John. *Poems.* Ed. Berdan. New York, 1903.

_________. *Poems.* Ed. Morris and Withington. Oxford, 1967.

Collier, J. Payne. *A Bibliographical and Critical Account of the Rarest Books in the English Language.* New York, 1866.

Cornwallis, Sir Charles. *The Life and Death of Our Most Incomparable and Heroique Prince Henry Prince of Wales.* London, 1641.

Coryat, Thomas. *Coryat's Crudities.* 2 vols. Glasgow, 1905.

Crashaw, Richard. *Poems.* Ed. L. C. Martin. Oxford, 1957.

Davies of Hereford, John. *Complete Works.* Ed. Grosart. 2 vols. 1878.

________. *The Muses Teares.* London, 1613.

Davies, Sir John. *Works in Verse and Prose.* 3 vols. n.p., 1869.

________. *Poems.* Ed. Clare Howard. New York, 1941.

Dodd, Henry P. *The Epigrammatists.* London, 1876.

Donne, John. *Poems.* Ed. H. J. C. Grierson. 2 vols. Oxford, 1912.

Draper, John W. *A Century of Broadside Elegies.* London, 1928.

________. *The Funeral Elegy and the Rise of English Romanticism.* New York, 1929.

Drayton, Michael. *Poems.* Ed. John Buxton. 2 vols. London, 1953.

________. *Works.* Ed. Hebel. 5 vols. Oxford, 1931–41.

Drummond, William. *Poems.* 2 vols. London and New York, 1894.

________. *Poetical Works.* Ed. L. E. Kastner. 2 vols. Manchester, 1913.

Fenton, John. *King James. His Welcome to London.* London, 1603.

Fletcher, Giles and Phineas. *Poetical Works.* Ed. Boas. 2 vols. Cambridge, England, 1908–9.

Freeman, Rosemary. *English Emblem Books.* London, 1948.

Gorges, Sir Arthur. *The Olympian Catastrophe.* Kensington, 1925.

Greek Anthology, The. Loeb Classical Library. Trans. W. R. Paton. 5 vols. London and New York, 1917–26.

________. Ed. George Burges. London, 1893.

________. Ed. A. S. F. Gow and D. L. Page. 2 vols. Cambridge, England, 1965.

Greene, Robert. *Plays and Poems.* Ed. J. C. Collins. 2 vols. Oxford, 1905.

Guilpin, Everard. *Skialetheia.* London, 1598.

________. *Skialetheia.* London, 1598. Reprint ed., Oxford, 1931.

Hannay, Patrick. *Poetical Works.* London, 1622. Reprint ed., 1875.

Harington, Sir John. *The Epigrams of Sir John Harington.* Ed. N. E. McClure. Philadelphia, 1926.

Harrison, T. P., Jr. *The Pastoral Elegy: An Anthology.* Austin, Texas, 1939.

Hawkins, Sir John. *Generall History of the Science and Practice of Music.* 5 vols. London, 1776.

Herbert of Cherbury, Edward. *Poems.* Oxford, 1923.

Heywood, John. *The Proverbs and Epigrams of John Heywood.* 2 vols. London, 1867.

Heywood, Thomas. *A Funerall Elegie, Upon the Death of the Late Most Hopefull and illustrious Prince, Henry, Prince of Wales.* London, 1613.

________. *A Marriage Triumph.* London, 1842.

Hudson, H. H. *The Epigram in the English Renaissance.* Princeton, 1947.

James, King. *Basilicon Doron.* London, 1599.

James, Richard. *Poems.* Ed. Grosart. Printed for private circulation, 1880.

Jenkins, Harold. *Life and Works of Henry Chettle.* London, 1934.

Jonson, Ben. *Epigrams, The Forest, Underwoods.* New York, 1936.

________. *Poems.* Ed. Newdigate. Oxford, 1936.

Justa Edovardo King Naufrago. Cambridge, England, 1638.

Kendall, Timothe. *Flowers of Epigrammes.* 1577. Reprint ed., London, 1874.

King, Henry. *Poems.* Ed. Margaret Crum. Oxford, 1965.

King James: His Welcome to London. London, 1603.

Lane, John. *Fugitive Poetical Tracts.* 2nd series, Roxburghe Library, n.d.

Levitt, Harold. "The Political Writings of Henry Peacham." New York University thesis, 1968.

Mackail, John William. *Select Epigrams from the Greek Anthology.* London and New York, 1906.

Martial. *The Epigrams of Martial.* London, 1897.

________. *Martial's Epigrams.* 2 vols. Cambridge, Mass., 1950.

Maxwell, James. *The Laudable Life, and Deplorable Death of Our Late Peerlesse Prince Henrie.* London, 1612.

________. *A Monument of Remembrance.* London, 1613.

Moorman, F. W. *Robert Herrick: A Biographical and Critical Study.* London and New York, 1910.

Nixon, Paul. *Martial and the Modern Epigram.* New York, 1927.

Pastoral Elegy, The: An Anthology. Ed. T. P. Harrison, Jr., Austin, Texas, 1939.

Peacham, Henry, Sr. *The Garden of Eloquence.* London, 1577.

Peacham, Henry, Jr. *A Most True Relation of the Affaires of Cleve and Gulick.* London, 1615.

________. *An Aprill Shower.* London, 1624.

________. *The Art of Drawing with the Pen, and Limming in Water Colours.* London, 1606.

________. *The Art of Living in London.* London, 1642.

________. *The Art of Living in London.* Included by V. B. Heltzel in his volume *Complete Gentleman,* etc. Ithaca, New York, 1962.

________. *Basilicon Doron.* Three ms. copies. Two in the British Museum (Ms. Harleian 6855 [13] and Ms. Royal 12 A. LXVI) and one in the Bodleian at Oxford (Mss. Rawlinson. p. 146).

________. *A Caution to Keepe Money.* London, 1642. Alternate title for *Worth of a Peny.*

________. *Coach and Sedan.* London, 1636.

________. *Coach and Sedan*. London, 1925.

________. *The Compleat Gentleman*. London, 1622.

________. *The Compleat Gentleman*. Ed. G. S. Gordon, Oxford, 1906.

________. *The Complete Gentleman and Other Works*. Ed. V. B. Heltzel, Ithaca, New York, 1962.

________. *A Dialogue Between The Crosse in Cheap, and Charing Crosse*. London, 1641.

________. *The Duty of All True Subjects to Their King: As also to their Native Countrey*. London, 1639.

________. *The Gentleman's Exercise* (alternate title for *Graphicé*). London, 1612.

________. *Graphicé, Or The Most Auncient and Excellent Art of Drawing and Limming*. London, 1612.

________. *A Merry Discourse of Meum and Tuum*. London, 1639.

________. *Minerva Britanna or a Garden of Heroical Devises*. London, 1612.

________. *Minerva Britanna*. Reprint ed., Menston, 1969.

________. *The More the Merrier*, London, 1608.

________. *Nuptiall Hymnes, in Honour of the Marriage of Princess Elizabeth and Count Palatine*. Printed with *The Period of Mourning*, London, 1613.

________. *A Paradox in the Praise of a Dunce, to Smectymnuus*. London, 1642.

________. *The Period of Mourning. Disposed into sixe Visions, In Memorie of the late Prince • Together with Nuptiall Hymnes*. London, 1613.

________. *The Period of Mourning*. London, 1789.

________. *Prince Henrie Revived*. London, 1615.

________. *Square-Caps Turned Into Round-Heads: Or The Bishops Vindication, And the Brownists Conviction*. London, 1642.

________. *Thalia's Banquet: Furnished with an hundred and odde dishes of newly devised epigrammes*. London, 1620.

________. *Thestylis Atrata*. London, 1634.

________. *The Truth of Our Times: Revealed out of one Mans Experience, by way of Essay*. London, 1638.

________. *The Truth of Our Times*. Ed. R. R. Cawley. New York, 1942.

________. *The Valley of Varietie*. London, 1638.

________. *The Worth of a Peny*. London, 1641?

________. *The Worth of a Penny*. London, 1677.

Pitman, Margaret C. "The Epigrams of Henry Peacham and Henry Parrot." *MLR*, XXIX (1934), 129–36.

________. "Studies in the Works of Henry Peacham," London University thesis, 1933.

Quarles, Francis. *Complete Works in Prose and Verse*. 3 vols. Ed. Grosart. 1880.

Spenser, Edmund. *Complete Poetical Works*. Ed. R. E. Neil Dodge. Cambridge, Mass., 1908.

________. *Works.* Ed. Greenlaw, Osgood, Padelford. Baltimore, 1932–.

Surrey, Henry Howard. *Poems.* Oxford, 1964.

Sylvester, Joshua, *Complete Works,* 2 vols. Edinburgh, 1880.

Symonds, J. A. *Studies of the Greek Poets,* London, 1902.

Taylor, John. *Works.* London, 1869, 1873.

Thynne, Francis. *Emblemes and Epigrames.* Ed. F. J. Furnivall, London, 1876.

Tourneur, Cyril. *Works.* Ed. Allardyce Nicoll. London, 1929.

Turberville, George. *Epithaphes, Epigrams, Songs and Sonets.* London, 1567.

Waller, Edmund. *Poems.* Ed. G. Thorn Drury. London and New York, 1893.

Wallerstein, Ruth. *Studies in Seventeenth-Century Poetic.* Madison, Wis., 1950.

Webster, John. *Works.* Ed. Alexander Dyce. London, 1857.

________. *Complete Works,* ed. F. L. Lucas. 4 vols. London, 1927.

Weever, John. *Epigrammes in the Oldest Cut and Newest Fashion.* 1599. Reprint ed., edited by R. B. McKerrow. Stratford, 1922.

Weitzmann, F. W. "Notes on the Elizabethan *Elegie,*" *PMLA, L,* 435–43.

Whipple, T. K. *Martial and the English Epigram from Sir Thomas Wyatt to Ben Jonson.* Berkeley, Calif., 1925.

Whitney, Geoffrey. *Choice of Emblems,* London, 1586.

Wilson, Elkin C. *Prince Henry and English Literature.* Ithaca, New York, 1946.

Wither, George. *Poems. Juvenilia.* London, 1871.

INDEX